Does God Still Guide?

Books by DR. J. SIDLOW BAXTER

AWAKE MY HEART
A devotional Bible study for every day in the year.

DOES GOD STILL GUIDE?
An answer to this important question in our time.

EXPLORE THE BOOK
A basic, progressive, interpretative course of Bible study, six volumes in one, from Genesis to Revelation.

GOD SO LOVED
An exposition of John 3:16, the best-known text in the Bible.

GOING DEEPER
A series of devotional studies in knowing, loving, and serving our Lord Jesus Christ.

HIS DEEPER WORK IN US
A further enquiry into New Testament teaching on the subject of Christian Holiness.

HIS PART AND OURS
Enriching exposition and devotional studies in the reciprocal union of Christ and His people.

MARK THESE MEN
Arresting studies of little understood aspects of Bible characters with special relevance for our times.

RETHINKING OUR PRIORITIES
A heart-to-heart talk with the church: its pastor and people.

STRATEGIC GRASP OF THE BIBLE
The marvelous design and structure of the Scriptures, with a discussion of the dispensational characteristics of biblical revelation.

STUDIES IN PROBLEM TEXTS
The problem texts of the Bible in patient and painstaking investigation.

CHRISTIAN HOLINESS: RESTUDIED AND RESTATED
Three works on the scriptural teaching on personal holiness, combined in one volume: *A New Call to Holiness, His Deeper Work in Us, Our High Calling*. These three are also available individually.

Does God Still Guide?

The Essentials of Guidance and Growth in the Christian Life

J. Sidlow Baxter

KREGEL PUBLICATIONS
Grand Rapids, Michigan 49501

Does God Still Guide?, © 1968 by J. Sidlow
Baxter. Published by special arrangement with
the author in 1991 by Kregel Publications, a division of Kregel, Inc., P. O. Box 2607, Grand Rapids,
MI 49501. All rights reserved.

Cover Photo: Art Jacobs
Cover Design: Al Hartman

ISBN 0-8254-2199-3 (pbk.)

1 2 3 4 5 Printing/Year 95 94 93 92 91

Printed in the United States of America

DEDICATION

With warm appreciation the following chapters
are dedicated to my gifted friend,

THE REVEREND SAMUEL M. FORSTER,
TH.M.,

than whom no minister of the Word ever had
a truer, kindlier, or more self-forgetting helper.

CONTENTS

FOREWORD

IF there is one thing more than another which our tense and nervous age needs, it is a guidance more than human. Today, scientific brilliance and spiritual blindness are a frightening union. By its restless cleverness the human brain has brought upon us a world situation just about beyond the limits of its own competence to control. Never was the question more anxiously asked: "Where are we going?"

But the international scene is simply a photograph of the individual heart in big enlargement. Man in the aggregate is but the bigger, bolder portrait of man in the singular. With either aching fear or sadness, countless hearts today keep asking, "Which is the right way? What's at the end? Is there a sure guide? Does *God* still guide? How may I know?"

The Bible answer is: Yes, there *is* guidance. God *offers* it to godly men and godly nations; and they may live safely in it. That is the subject of this book—particularly in its reference to the godly *individual*. It is written with intentional simplicity, yet I dare to hope that it may possibly give useful direction to some, at least, who read it. Dear reader, if it only brings as much challenge to you in *reading* it as it did to me in *writing* it, that will have made it well worthwhile.

J. S. B.

PART ONE

ASPECTS OF GUIDANCE

GUIDANCE: WHY WE NEED IT

"The basic struggle is for the wills of men. That is the ideological struggle. It goes on in your heart and mine, every day.
Armies and pacts and economic assistance are necessary; but the deciding factor is whether, as men and nations, we are guided by the voice of materialism or by the voice of God."

Frank Buchman.

"He that planted the ear, shall He not hear? He that formed the eye, shall He not see?"

Psalm 94: 9.

"He telleth the number of the stars. He healeth the broken in heart."

Psalm 147: 3, 4.

1

GUIDANCE: WHY WE NEED IT

THE question, "Does God still guide?" presupposes, of course, that God *is*. Today, if I decipher the times aright, belief in God needs no apology, but only new emphasis. That vain, human conceit which at the beginning of our twentieth century said, "Modern science and scholarship can comfortably dispense with belief in God," was far more naive than the godly simplicity at which it sneered. Where have twentieth-century science, discovery, invention and education landed us? Robert Maynard Hutchins, recently president at the University of Chicago, has said, "We do not know where we are going, or why, and we have almost given up the attempt to find out. We are in despair because the keys which were to open the gates of heaven have let us into a larger but more oppressive prison-house. We thought these keys were science and the free intelligence of man. *They have failed us.* We have long since cast off God. To what can we now appeal?"

The boast of godless science has now become the heart-sob of a clever creature who has lost his way in the dark, near fearful precipices; a clever creature able to master many secrets of the physical universe, but utterly unable to master the enigmatical contrariety and perversity of his own moral nature; too self-sufficient to accept guidance from divine Revelation, yet too erring and sinful to find his own way back to saving truth. Never before has there been such brilliantly educated godlessness, boredom, crime, unchastity, and, along with it all, in millions of hearts, a wearying sense of being lost in an existence which seems to have no dignified meaning.

If there is one thing more than another today which misled nations, leaders and people need—and many ache to find, it is moral and spiritual *guidance*; that guidance which comes only through divine revelation and regeneration, i.e. through the Holy Scriptures and the Holy Spirit.

Meanwhile, those of us who have *found* the way of true guidance keep lifting up our voice in testimony to it, hoping that at least

some will hear us. We do this with more eagerness just now because we seem to detect that today, more than for a long while,
there are wistful minds all around us asking, no longer with con-
tempt but with concern, *DOES GOD STILL GUIDE?*

The answer given in these unpretentious studies is Scriptural,
not philosophical. It is no sophisticated defence of our Christian
position, but a designedly practical exposition of divine guidance
in individual human life, as taught in Scripture and exemplified
in human experience. For my own part, I believe that the Biblical
approach to such a subject is always the *safest* as well as the
simplest. Therefore my prayerful hope can be that the ensuing
pages may bring constructive comment and encouragement
to any reader whose earnest question is, *DOES GOD STILL
GUIDE?*

But there is another reason why this matter of divine guidance
keeps knocking at my door, and claiming new attention. During
my preaching and lecturing travels in various parts of the world
these past twelve years or so, no question has been asked more
often of me by Christian believers than these: How can I know
the will of God for my life? How can I know the will of God in
some particular situation? How can I *experience* divine guidance?
How does such guidance come? How do I recognise it? How can
I be really *sure* of it? When we reflect how vast the universe is,
and how infinitesimal one tiny human entity is by comparison,
does it not seem absurdly gratuitous to suppose that God separ-
ately guides the way for any *one* such evanescent fleck of spray
on the vast ocean of existence?

These questions have been asked of us by Christian believers
of varying age, of all denominations, of all social levels, and of
all stages in Christian experience. They are evidently questions
of keen concern to very many. Each will come up for considera-
tion in these pages; but maybe we ought to halt at the last-men-
tioned one right away. It is based upon a mistaken idea of God,
of the universe, and of human beings.

To a God who is *infinite,* there can be no such distinctions as
"big" or "little". Every "detail" (so-called by *our* finite minds)
down to the smallest (as judged by us) is to God a *necessary* part
of the magnificent whole. To a God who is *eternal* there can be
neither past nor future; all is a transparent, continuous, *now,*
right down to the present tick of our human clocks. God does not

love this planet of ours for its physical bigness or littleness. What is mere physical size to a God who creates Orion and Pleiades and the Milky Way? If God has a special love for this world of ours it *must* be for some reason far above the merely physical.

As always, in such matters, the Bible has the answer. God loves this world, not for its mere material bulk, but for its *moral value*. On this earth are millions upon millions of human souls, the posterity of a human "original" with a mental and moral nature made in the very "image" and "likeness" of God. That "image" and "likeness", though long distorted through the intrusion of sin and its continuing hereditary consequences, is still there. Unlike all other beings in his cosmic environment, man is *capax Dei*, "capable of God".

When the scientist scans the skies through his latest telescope and tells us that "astronomically speaking" man is too little even to be noticed, we may well repeat that "astronomically speaking" man is the *astronomer*! The biggest alpha-star of the universe is blind. It can be seen but it cannot see. It can be weighed and measured and analysed, but it cannot think or know or feel. It can be admired but it cannot worship (or rebel) or love (or hate) or adore (or defy). Little man is immeasurably bigger than the biggest telescope he ever makes; and the little human mind which peers through that big telescope is bigger far than anything which the telescope swings into view. As poet Edward Young says—

> How poor, how rich, how abject, how august,
> How complicate, how wonderful, is man!
> How passing wonder He who made him such!
> Who centred in our make such strange extremes!
> From different natures marvellously mix'd,
> Connection exquisite of distant worlds!
> Distinguished link in being's endless chain!
> Midway from nothing to the Deity!
> A beam ethereal, sullied and absorbed!
> Though sullied and dishonoured still divine!
> Dim miniature of greatness absolute!
> An heir of glory! a frail child of dust!
> Helpless immortal! insect infinite!
> A worm! a god!—I tremble at myself,
> And in myself am lost! At home a stranger,
> Thought wanders up and down, surprised, aghast,
> And wondering at her own: how reason reels!
> O what a miracle to man is man,
> Triumphantly distressed! what joy, what dread!

Alternately transported and alarmed!
What can preserve my life, or what destroy?
No angel's arm can snatch me from the grave;
Nor angel legions can confine me there!

Our modern geologists may tell us that the age of this earth is some three thousand million years; that our human existence here is the mere flap of a bird's wing; and that the very idea of our having fellowship with the titanic Architect of the universe is preposterous; but there is another side to all that. There is the witness of that wonderful Book which not only *claims* to be the authentic Word of God, but *proves* to be so by scientific tests just as sound as those of the geologist. There is the witness of honest, rational, logical evidence from numberless human testifiers. A tree may be five hundred times bigger than a man and may live three thousand years. A man lives only seventy or eighty years, and his little body drops into a grave. So, is the tree greater? When a tree dies it is dead and done for ever. When a man dies he merely discards a mortal body to live in a Beyond with an endless destiny.

Although living in time, man was made for eternity. "He [God] has put eternity into man's mind" (Eccles. 3: 11, R.S.V.). For six millenniums from Adam downwards, men have lived, laboured, learned, laughed, wept and died on this earth, and upon finally closing their eyes here have wakened in Sheol, or Hades, in the mysterious Beyond where man's ultimate destiny lies. Today, there are two thousand million such God-conscious souls on this spinning orb—each responsible to God, each capable of love or hate, of heaven or hell; each with a vast destiny beyond the strange gates of the grave. Not only is the physical universe blind and deaf, it is dumb. Man can *speak!* He can both listen and talk to God! He can hold *fellowship* with God! He was made for that very purpose! Satan has tricked him. Sin has defiled him. He can suffer for ages in Gehenna! But he can be *saved!* Science is now rapidly on its way to showing us that there is *no* sentient life on Venus or Mars—or on the other planets of our solar system. Man is unique. Science is going to tell us in a new way and despite itself, why "God so loved *this* world that He gave His only-begotten Son, that whosoever believeth in Him should not perish, but have everlasting life."

Yes, this world of ours is unique in our solar system. It is the only planet peopled with God-conscious minds living in bodies. It is unspeakably dear to the boundless heart of God. Every human being is of unspeakable concern to Him. *You* are! *I* am! The supreme demonstration of it is that God the Son Himself entered our humanhood on this earth by a real human birth—that greatest mystery of time or eternity—in order to redeem us with His "precious blood", and break the grip of the arch-deceiver. If God incarnate would wear that jagged crown and hang on that gory cross, impaled by iron spikes, and endure the torture of that fearful agony for *our* sakes, then, oh, how God *must* love us! Let doubt of Him now hang its head in deepest shame. Who can want more trustworthy evidence that Christ is indeed incarnate God than the combined prophetic and historic witness of both Hebrew and Christian Scriptures? As for the wonder that God indeed *loves* us, sinners though we are, who can dare ask for more lavish proof than that "wonderful Cross" supplies?

> See, from His head, His hands, His feet,
> Sorrow and love flow mingled down:
> Did e'er such love and sorrow meet,
> Or thorns compose so rich a crown?

In the light of all the evidence (evidence which has been doubted, tested, and vindicated a thousand times) who needs go on doubting the reality of the Saviour's *resurrection*? Or, in the miraculous character-transformation of the Apostles, who can fail to see that the *Spirit* of God really came to infill those men on the historic "Day of Pentecost"? Marvel again at the depthless wonder of it—all the Triunity of the Godhead involved in man's salvation. God, as the all-Sovereign *Father*—loving and giving! God as the incarnate *Saviour*—dying and saving! God as the indwelling Spirit—filling and guiding!

That is the shining mystery and rich reality of the New Testament teaching: the Father *above* me—controlling all things: the Saviour *beside* me—directing my footsteps: the Spirit *within* me—impressing me inwardly. Those who doubt it all may well keep on dismally or incredulously asking, DOES GOD STILL GUIDE? But those of us who know it all to be true, how can *we* ever again doubt that God guides? He has actually come to live with us and within us for that purpose! The object of these pages is to answer with a grateful, joyful positive: YES, GOD DOES STILL GUIDE!

WHY WE NEED DIVINE GUIDANCE

So, then, on into our subject; and our first question is: Why do we *need* divine guidance? By "guidance" we mean divine direction for our living and doing as human *individuals*. Such guidance we all need, from the first glimmers of responsibility to the last dip of life's sun. Especially do we need divine guidance in spiritual concerns; for although man has contrived a scientific cleverness in things mathematical and material he remains hereditarily obtuse and gullible in spiritual matters. Although man's spiritual *instincts* are constitutionally ineradicable, the fact remains that whatever authenticated spiritual *knowledge* he now possesses has come, not by human discovery, but by divine revelation.

That leads to a further preliminary observation. Through the written Word of God, and the incarnate Son of God, divine revelation has already given us an all-sufficient *general* guidance in matters moral and spiritual; a guidance which covers, in principle, all the moral and spiritual choices, crises, issues and obligations of our earthly life; a guidance adequate to ensure our individual salvation, our fundamental well-being in this present life, and our enduring felicity in the next. If only we all lived according to the precepts and principles, the admonitions and exhortations, of the Holy Word, what nobility, serenity, consistence, and solid consolations would be ours!

Wonderful, however, as is this over-all Biblical directory, most of us, as we encounter our daily life, feel the need for *direct* guidance from above, a guidance amid particular problems which no static book-guidance could specifically cover. We need this guidance, not *instead* of the Bible, but *along* with it.

Some years ago, on a voyage from Vancouver, B.C., to New Zealand, I noticed that all the way from Victoria to the Hawaiian Islands the captain of our vessel never once missed taking his meals with us in the dining hall; not until we neared Suva, capital of the Fiji Islands; then his chair became vacant. I asked one of the stewards why, and he replied: "So far, all the way over the Pacific we have been guided by Radar; but now that we are approaching Suva the captain needs to be on the bridge. There is an under-water coral reef which now leaves only a half-mile gap through which to enter the harbour. We daren't trust to Radar here; the captain himself needs to guide from the bridge." Similarly, the Bible is our God-given radar for life's seas in general; but again and again there are reefs and Suvas where we need the Captain Himself on the bridge to give us His own immediate guidance.

It is a precious fact that the Holy Scripture *promises* such individual guidance to us, "if we walk in the light as He is in the light". "I will instruct thee, and teach thee in the way which thou shalt go; I will guide thee with Mine eye upon thee" (Ps. 32: 8). "Jehovah shall guide thee continually" (Isa. 58: 11); "Thine ears shall hear a word behind thee, saying, This is the way; walk ye in it" (Isa. 30: 21). "When he, the Spirit of truth, is come, he will guide you . . ." (John 16: 13). "As many as are led by the Spirit of God, they are the sons of God" (Rom. 8: 14). None of these means a guidance *instead* of the written Word, but as a companion and complement of it.

The very fact that Scripture repeatedly promises this guidance carries the implication that we need it. Many of us are more or less aware of needing it; yet few, I suspect, discern the *deeper* necessities for it. Why are prayers often left ungranted? It is because, with many of us, the real need is not for answers to our present requests, so much as a complete change in our motives, desires, and askings. Why does divine guidance often seem withheld or obscure? It is because, if truly spiritual guidance came, many of us would scarcely recognise it, or feel able to follow it. The truth is, that far too often what we are asking is guidance for self-management, whereas the guidance which God would fain give us is guidance to do *His Will*; for that alone fulfils His highest intent and our own highest good. Admittedly, guidance often *does* come to us amid well-meant self-management; for God sees that the motive is sincere so far as it goes; but the guidance is *accommodated* rather than top-level communication.

We Christians are meant to be not only Christocentric, but Christo*cratic*. Christ is meant to be not only the centre of our being, but the Disposer of our life. Every regenerated personality is meant to be a Christocracy; a threefold territory of spirit, soul and body under the absolute sceptre of Christ. Most of us, however, although we are unboundedly grateful to be saved from the damnation of Gehenna, through the precious blood of Christ, prefer to have Him only as a "constitutional monarch" in which our own parliament makes the laws and then gets the king to homologate them. Under such a regime, autosuggestion is often louder than the voice from the throne; real guidance is either blocked or blurred.

We need divine guidance because *God knows our nature as no one else does*. When some of us were little boys it was fashionable for mothers to take their young sons to a phrenologist, to see what they were best fitted for. The phrenologist would professionally finger cranial bumps and dents, and thereby interpret a boy's aptitudes and abilities. Nowadays, the vogue is to consult a psychologist or some other kindred specialist. I will not rashly criticise this procedure; there may be real usefulness in such consultations; but I make bold to assert that they are a poor substitute for divine guidance,

What was it the discerning psalmist said? "Thine eyes did see my substance, yet being unperfect; and in Thy book all my members were written when as yet there was none of them." No one else knows us in that way! That is the psychology of Omniscience. I recall how God said to Jeremiah, "Before I formed thee . . . I knew thee; and before thou camest forth . . . I sanctified thee, and ordained thee a prophet unto the nations". I remember, too, how Jesus said to Simon, "Thou art Simon, the son of Jona: thou shalt be called Cephas, which is by interpretation, a stone" (John 1: 42). Our Lord Jesus is the divine Wisdom looking inside us through human eyes. It is written of Him, "Jesus . . . needed not that any should testify of man: for He knew what was in man." He knows, as no other, all our propensities and possibilities; what we should do, and where we should be. Let the younger among us realise that He guides careers as well as transforms character; and let the older among us reflect that He guides in Autumn as well as in Spring. Both in life's earlier choices and in life's later changes, none can guide as He. Yes, we need divine guidance because God knows our nature as no one else does.

But again, we need divine guidance because *God knows the future as no one else does*. Ours is the age of scientific knowing rather than philosophic reasoning; but there is one thing which modern man does not and cannot know, any more than his predecessors; that is *the future*. We may guess or prognosticate, but we cannot fore*see*; and what need for divine guidance *this* imposes!

How acute in the days of youth is the need for such guidance!

Youth is a time of wonderful nerve and naivete. We do things with a gay risk for which we suffer all our lives. What sad illustrations could be given! Take marriage, for instance. What tragedies there are because wedlock is contracted without divine guidance! Married life can be either a "heaven below" or a "hell on earth"; it can be either a life-long comfort or a life-long sorrow; and parenthood can be either a paradise or a prison. Next to the salvation of the soul through conversion to Christ, love and wedlock are the most sacred and serious and determinative of all factors in adult life; yet how often they end in ugly tragedy or embittering disillusionment because of foolish choice or false guidance! How often, for the same reason, people draw near to the end of life's earthly span with Disraeli's dirge on their lips:

> "Youth is a mistake;
> Manhood a struggle;
> Old age a regret."

Years ago, when the famous American evangelist, Dwight L. Moody, met the intellectual English prime minister, W. E. Gladstone, the slim, aristocratic-looking Gladstone said to the young, broad-built Moody, "I wish I had your shoulders"; and Moody quickly countered, "I wish I had your head on them". There is a plaintive adage which says, "You cannot put old heads on young shoulders". Nor can you; but what is far more needed than either a Gladstone head or Moody shoulders is the guidance of God. He alone knows the future; and He alone can give us that guidance *today* which safeguards *tomorrow*.

Once again, we need divine guidance because *God has a purpose for each of us such as no one else has*. One of the most arresting and dignifying truths of Scripture revelation is, that for every human being there is a preconceived divine plan and intention. There are many people today who are sceptical of this because the universe is so vast and mortal man so infinitesimally unnoticeable, or because history seems like a huge, rolling juggernaut which crushes humanity's millions beneath its inexorable wheels with contemptuous disregard of individual considerations. Also, of course, the evolutionist philosophies and dictator-totalitarianisms of our time view the earth's races as merely so many herds of human cattle rather than as individual beings made in the image of God. We have to make choice between those two concepts: either each human being represents an individual instance of divine purpose, or we are just millions and millions of meaningless accidents. If the former is true, our world is a providential *kosmos* with a good purpose. If the latter is true, then all is a savage *chaos* plunging on into a nameless inferno.

Thank God, the Holy Scriptures, along with enlightened human experience and many other scientifically sound factors, are all against the evolutionist and collectivist aberrations. We discern the image of God on the brow of each human being, however distorted that image often may be. We human beings are incidents, not accidents. We are significant, not irrelevant. We are dear to our Maker; and He has a purpose for each of us; a purpose which not only spans our present, fleeting earth-life, but reaches on beyond the grave to an intended destiny out-bounding all reckonings of time.

We recall again God's words to Jeremiah, "Before I formed thee . . . I knew thee: and before thou camest forth . . . I set thee apart, and I ordained thee a prophet unto the nations". But this onreaching purpose of God does not only include prophets, it even takes in poor, blind, roadside beggars! In John's Gospel, chapter 9, the disciples ask Jesus, "Master, who did sin, this man or his parents, that he was born blind?" Our Lord gave this astonishing reply, "Neither hath this man sinned nor his parents: but [this is] that the works of God should be made manifest in him. I must work the works of Him that sent me, while it is day. . . ." Before ever he was born, that human soul was in the divine purpose, to become a wonderful testimonial to all succeeding generations, of the Saviour's transforming power! We think also of Ephesians 2: 10, "For we are His workmanship [lit. 'poem'], created in Christ Jesus unto good works, which God hath before ordained [or prepared] that we should walk in them."

I would say to our *younger* people: Get into God's plan for your life without delay. Your mother, your father, your teacher, your closest confidants, may each have a conviction as to how you should shape your years, and in greater or lesser degree they may, or may not, coincide with the *divine* intention for you; but the *vital* thing is to know and fulfil *God's* pattern for your life. Also, I would say to our *older* folk: If through the past years you have *missed* the intended divine "original" for this earthly chapter, then however understandable may be your tears of regret, do not let regret become fatalistic despair. Remember that the divine plan reaches on into the eternal future, and God is the

Master-Adapter who can overrule, improvise, re-fashion, and eventually bring about the pre-intended ultimate by an alternative route. Give yourself to Him with utter unreserve. By so doing, *you* will get back into His over-all purpose, and *He* will begin at once to shape your remaining years on earth in accord with His larger intentions for you in that endless destiny beyond.

There is a compassionate *adaptability* about God's will for us, in a way which many of us need to realise more clearly. Because we have not been in God's special will for us from the beginning, there is no reason why we should not get into it *now*. He can take up from where we get right.

One of the dearest friends my wife and I ever had was a "mother in Israel" who in her younger years had received a distinct "call" to the overseas mission field, and had deliberately said "No" to God. She was much in love with a fine young man, and was not willing to forgo marriage for the sake of the mission field. Marriage brought unexpected griefs, including the husband's long drawn-out suffering and death by cancer. But, most of all, she was now broken by a sense of the awful wrong she had committed in deliberately going out of the will of God. For a time there was blank despair. Then she realised that an all-foreknowing heavenly Father must surely have *alternative* avenues of service for such as herself who come back in deep contrition. She really got back into the will of God again; not into the original blueprint of overseas missionary service, but into an alternative design which was waiting for the rest of her time on earth. She gave herself up to Christ, to do His will as He should reveal it. Her master-motto was, "Whatsoever He saith unto you, do it". She became the greatest soul-winner I have ever known among women. Sunday after Sunday, during the Second World War, she would bring in a dozen or more soldiers, sailors, airmen, or service-women to our Gospel meetings. Scores of them she herself led to Christ. When she celebrated her eightieth birthday I was a guest speaker; and I am not exaggerating when I say that her face and personality on that occasion eradiated the presence of Christ. The great thing is for you and me to get into the special plan and purpose of God for us now. It is not too late. Remember, this present life is only the beginning.

Meanwhile, these are the three main reasons why we need divine guidance: (1) God knows our nature as no one else does. (2) God knows the future as no one else does. (3) God has a purpose for us such as no one else has. Thank God, we not only *need* guidance, but, according to clear promise, we may *have* it if we sincerely seek it.

> Oh, blest relief for harried heart and mind,
> Such teachings in the dear old Book to find!
> Mid shifting sands of men's philosophies,
> To have this Rock of solid certainties!
> Could God Himself give mightier guarantee
> Than bleed, incarnate, on a Cross for me?
> Why need I longer doubt that Love Divine?—
> The blood-sealed promises are truly mine!
> All-seeing Mind each human pathway scans,
> And pure Benevolence foresees, foreplans:
> Why doubt this depthless mystery of Grace?
> God pre-designs for each some special place:
> Oh, let me learn my heavenly Father's will,
> And seek His all-wise purpose to fulfil!
> *That, that alone, is life lived at its best;*
> *And that alone gives human hearts true rest.*
>
> But can that plan include the dull routine
> Of daily chores, oft-seeming trivial, mean?—
> The office desk, the factory, the store,
> Those thousand-times-repeated jobs galore?
> Blest is the man indeed who learns to find
> The heavenly with the earthly intertwined!
> Who sees in mundane chores a graded school,
> And all this life on earth a vestibule
> To bigger, grander, higher destiny
> In yonder realm of immortality!
> For true it is: our Maker's master-plan
> Includes each day and hour of every man:
> Yes, let me learn my heavenly Father's will,
> And seek His all-wise purpose to fulfil!
> *That, that alone, is life lived at its best;*
> *And that alone gives human hearts true rest.*

WHEN DOES GUIDANCE COME?

"I, being in the way, Jehovah led me."
Genesis 24: 27.

"Ye shall seek Me, and find Me, when ye shall search for Me with all your heart."
Jeremiah 29: 13.

"Our power to perceive the light of God is, of all our powers, the one which we need most to cultivate and develop. As exercise strengthens the body and education enlarges the mind, so the spiritual faculty within us grows as we use it in seeing and doing God's will."
Friends' Book of Discipline.

2

WHEN DOES GUIDANCE COME?

ALL of us Christian believers are aware of our need for divine guidance amid the choices and crises and issues of our daily life; and most of us are anxious to experience it; yet many of us are left wondering why it seems so uncertain or elusive. We want this guidance but somehow it does not seem operative. Why? Well, the fault usually lies at our own door. It is not that guidance is a discouragingly intricate matter, as is often wrongly supposed; it is in our own hearts that the deceptive intricacy exists. Away back in Jeremiah 17: 9, we read: "The heart is deceitful above all things, and desperately wicked." Therein lies the subtle reason why we are often self-cheated of divine guidance. It will be worthwhile to reflect on this. We can easily test ourselves by facing up to three requirements which all of us *can* fulfil if we *will*; three conditions which *must* be fulfilled if we are to experience clear direction from God.

No Known Sinful Way

It is surely obvious that we cannot reasonably expect divine guidance if we tolerate *sinful practices or unworthy ways* in our life. The Word says, "If any of you lack wisdom, let him ask of God . . . and it shall be given him" (Jas. 1: 5); but it also says, "If I regard iniquity in my heart, the Lord will not hear me" (Ps. 66: 18). God says, "I will instruct thee and teach thee in the way which thou shalt go: I will guide thee with mine eye upon thee" (Ps. 32: 8); but how can we get the guidance of that eye if we allow dark barriers of compromise to come between us and it? Many Christians who wonder why our Lord does not give them guidance have no real cause to wonder at all: the reason why it does not come is that they do not "walk in the light, as He is in the light" (1 John 1: 7). Have you ever tried to direct somebody in the dark? Directions which would be easy to follow in the daylight are often bothersome at night. Is it to be wondered at that even God finds us difficult to guide clearly when we are not walking "in the light", with every unworthy way renounced?

A certain minister preached a sermon on "Christian Separation". In it he touched on the habit of tobacco smoking. One of his church members afterwards remarked, "I'd never give up smoking for *him*". The remark was an all-too-common camouflage of insincerity, for the issue was not merely between that man and his minister, but between himself and God who had challenged him through the minister. In contrast to this, the Reverend Tydeman Chilvers, who for some twenty years conducted a mighty ministry at Spurgeon's Tabernacle in London, once told me that when he was seeking guidance, years before, about taking up the work at the Tabernacle, it seemed as though guidance simply would not come, however hard he prayed for it. Instead, every time he knelt in prayer, the matter of his pipe came up (he was a heavy smoker). At last he said, "Lord, if this thing displeases Thee, then, hard as it will be to break off, I renounce it for Thy dear sake." Immediately thereupon the longed-for guidance broke through like a bright sunshaft on a cloudy day.

We do not mention smoking because of any exclusive bearing which it may have on this subject of divine guidance, but simply because the two instances just cited illustrate how *any* such habit, or other point of controversy between the soul and Christ, may frustrate guidance. Let it be settled in our minds once for all, that clear guidance never comes where there is compromise with the unholy or questionable.

One of the things which used to shock me as a young Christian minister was the derogatory gossip indulged in by groups of ministers or other Christian workers, often under the guise of Christian "fellowship". A certain pattern became apparent to me. The Reverend So-and-so, or some other Christian leader would be mentioned. Complimentary remarks would be made first; then somebody would bring in the inevitable "But . . ." and from that point the cruel smearing or back-knifing would begin. Some of it was nothing less than scandal-mongering disguised as so-called "constructive criticism"! Eventually I made a vow (over thirty years ago now), *never* to criticise another evangelical minister behind his back. That vow has not spared *me* from being criticised —often wrongly, cruelly, and with no chance to reply, but it *has* spared me those wretched feelings of self-despising which follow after we have jealously or hurtfully defamed others; and it has saved me from one of those leading faults which becloud or completely *fog* divine guidance.

So long as we hug grudges, or relish cruel tittle-tattle, or harbour jealousies, or indulge dishonest exaggerations, or whisper confidential gossip-slanders, we disqualify ourselves from any real heart-to-heart fellowship with Christ, thus making His guidance of us quite impossible. Often it is not big, outward, obvious deviations which frustrate guidance, but these inward and covert compromises. We may well pray with the psalmist, "Cleanse Thou me from *secret* faults" (Ps. 19: 12).

There is such a thing as guidance *denied*. There came a point from which God refused to give His guiding word even to His covenant people. Through the prophet Ezekiel He says that "they have eyes to see, yet see not; they have ears to hear, yet hear not; for they are a rebellious house" (Ezek. 12: 2). So, where there is rebellion in the heart there cannot be guidance in the life. Controversy with God gives us eyes which see not and ears which hear not.

In another place God says through the same prophet, "These men have set up *idols in their heart*. . . . Should I be enquired of at all by them?" (14: 3). So, again, where there is some inward idolatry—some giving to a mere creature the love and devotion which belong to God alone, there cannot be divine guidance. Idolatry blinds just as surely as rebelliousness.

Thorough Sincerity

Again, there must be thorough *sincerity* in our seeking divine guidance. Sometimes an hour of honest heart-searching will expose a bent motive. Under guise of seeking to know *God's* will, what we are really wanting is God's corroboration of our *own*! There is a glaring instance of this in Jeremiah 42 and 43. After repeated forewarnings from Jehovah's faithful prophet, Jerusalem had at last fallen prey to the desolator. The emperor of Babylon had reduced the city to a tangled heap. The royal princes of Judah had been slain; the captured Judean king had been blinded and dragged in chains to Babylon. The bulk of the people had been carried captive into exile. Only a poverty-stricken few had been left in the land of Judah, among whom Jeremiah was permitted to stay. The Babylonian emperor, Nebuchadnezzar, appointed Gedaliah governor over those who were left in the land; but a certain Ishmael slew him and fled. The remainder, under the leadership of one named Johanan, purposed fleeing into Egypt, to escape the expected reprisal of Nebuchadnezzar. Before going, however, they thought it best to enquire for guidance of Jehovah; so they came to Jeremiah, and said,

"Let, we beseech thee, our supplication be accepted before thee, and pray for us unto Jehovah thy God, even for all this remnant (for we are left but a few of many, as thine eyes do behold us); that Jehovah thy God may show us the way wherein we may walk, and the thing we may do" (Jer. 42: 2, 3).

This seemed sincere enough; and they certainly needed special guidance in their predicament; so Jeremiah replied,

"I will pray unto Jehovah your God according to your words; and it shall come to pass, that whatsoever thing Jehovah shall answer you, I will declare it unto you; I will keep nothing back from you" (4).

To this, the enquiring remnant responded with a most impressive expression of good faith,

"Jehovah be a true and faithful witness between us, if we do not even according to all things for which Jehovah thy God shall send thee to us. Whether it be good, or whether it be evil, we will obey the voice of Jehovah our God, to whom we send thee; that it may be well with us, when we obey the voice of Jehovah our God" (5, 6).

Could any appeal for divine guidance have seemed sincerer? Yet when Jeremiah brought them the Lord's answer that they should not go to Egypt, but remain in Judea, this is what they said:

"Thou speakest falsely: Jehovah our God hath not sent thee to say, Go not into Egypt to sojourn there" (43: 2).
"As for the word that thou hast spoken unto us in the name of Jehovah, we will not hearken unto thee; but we will certainly do whatsoever thing goeth forth out of our own mouth" (44: 16, 17).

The fact is, those people were not genuinely seeking the divine will at all, but a corroboration of their own. Superficially, they thought that they *wanted* divine guidance as much as they *needed* it: but they were self-deceived. Deep down they wanted their own way, and were even angered when God disagreed! So is it often with ourselves, unless there is a penetrating self-scrutiny. These labyrinthine minds and hearts of ours can trick us into the subtle delusion that we want divine guidance when in reality what we want is divine approval of our own decisions. Guidance itself is no intricate problem; it is we ourselves who complicate it. When there is singleness of motive along with sincere seeking, the Holy Spirit makes His leading plain; but *not until* then.

Complete Obedience

Once again, if we are to live in the experience of continual guidance there must be continual obedience to God. To be guided we must be *controlled*. Ask any bronco which comes first—to guide a horse, or to control it. Ask any motorist which comes first—to guide a car, or to control it. All around us we see illustrations of this fact, that the prerequisite of guidance is *control*. Perhaps more than any other single factor, incomplete yieldedness to God cheats us of clear and continual guidedness.

A certain young woman had allowed herself to become emotionally entangled with a young man who could do her nothing but harm. Friends who felt deep concern for her tried to argue her out of her enchantment, but with no success. Then they besieged her on Scriptural grounds, and begged her not to go contrarily to the revealed will of God. At last they got her down on her knees to pray with them; and, with emotional gulps, she prayed, "Thy will . . . be done . . . O Lord . . . but *please* give me Jimmie!" Now I am sure that the Lord sympathises with us in our struggles against truant emotions and devious motives; yet His patient forbearance does not alter the fact that any kind of selfy "*but*" after "Thy will be done," more or less nullifies it, and lessens our susceptibility to real guidance. It smacks of Jacob-like bargaining with God—"If *God* will . . . then *I* will" (Gen. 28: 20, 21). Such bargainings with God are not true covenants at all, but self-manufactured imitations; and if God is to get us where He really *can* guide us, He often has to wrestle our thigh out of joint, as He eventually did with fertile-minded but self-deceived Jacob. On the other hand, when our life motto is that of the famous missionary, Arnot, "The will of God, nothing less, nothing more," *then* divine guidance becomes a luminous reality.

It seems strange to some of us that many Christians of the present generation have never even heard the name of George Müller. In the latter half of the nineteenth century George Müller founded the Bristol Orphan Homes, which later became famous all over the Christian world as one of the most remarkable monuments of human faith and divine faithfulness in history. Year after year, without a single advertisement to the public, and without a single appeal to Christian friends, hundreds of children were fed, clothed, educated, and the homes maintained, with all needs unfailingly met, simply in answer to prayer and faith. George Müller left us a significant testimony concerning this matter of divine guidance.

> "I never remember in all my Christian course (a period now of sixty-nine years and four months) that I ever sincerely and patiently sought to know the will of God by the teaching of the Holy Spirit, through the instrumentality of the Word, without being directed clearly and rightly. But if honesty of heart and uprightness before God were lacking, or if I did not patiently wait upon God for instruction, or if I preferred the counsel of my fellowmen to the declarations of the Word of the living God, I made great mistakes."

Never Given Where Needless

But now, even if we measure up to the foregoing requirements, are there *other* reasons why guidance sometimes does not come? Yes: and the main three are as follows.

First: "special" direction is never given when the guidance we ask is already *written in Scripture*. Although many directions concerning moral and social matters are clearly given in Holy Writ, some Christian believers seem to want supernatural visions or voices or verifications in addition. They are like long-ago Gideon, who, although he already had the word of God by special revelation, required two more signs: first he wanted his "fleece of wool" to be wet with dew, and all the ground dry; then his "fleece of wool" to be dry, and all the ground wet. God acceded to him because Gideon did not have the divine word in actual writing; but now that we Christian believers have the *written Word,* God no longer drenches or dries our "fleeces" in addition to what is written. Why does that Christian young woman keep begging God for guidance whether to marry an attractive but unconverted young man, when all the while the Word plainly says, "Be not unequally yoked together with unbelievers"? Why does that Christian businessman plead for a "sign" whether to clinch a profitable deal with a smirk in it, when the Word says, "Abstain from all appearance of evil"? No; guidance is not given where Scripture itself clearly guides us; it would be a superfluity.

Second: "special" guidance is never given when the guidance we ask is a *matter of plain duty*. If we know that we "ought" to do something, or to refrain from doing it, as a moral obligation, then to be asking special guidance is not a sign of spiritual-mindedness, but a symptom of spiritual weakliness. A classic instance of this is the prophet Balaam (Num. 22–24). When the messengers came to him from Balak, king of the Moabites, bringing him rich "rewards of divination", if he would curse the people of Israel, he knew at once that he should flatly refuse; yet with his eye on the rich payment he temporized, saying he must make it a matter of prayer! Scripture says that he "loved the wages of unrighteousness". In the end, he forfeited all reward, exasperated king Balak, incurred the anger of God, and became a monument of hypocrisy. Praying for "guidance" when duty is clear can lead to grave sins, deep delusions, and pathetic regrets. Such "praying" is a redundancy which the Holy Spirit never honours. If there is some step to take, some letter to write, some word to speak, in order to right a wrong, or some decision to make which according to all Christian principles is a moral "*I ought*", then the guidance we need is not *whether* to do it, but only the wisest *way* to do it.

Third: "special" guidance is never given as *a substitute for sanctified common sense*. Divine Guidance may sometimes cause us to do the unusual, but never the nonsensical or erratic. I know of a "very spiritual" woman who, again and again on the way to church, would suddenly have "guidance" to return home. In our public prayer-meetings we used to have a "very earnest" brother who would "feel led" to pray about such intimate and puerile matters that all the rest of us would blush or writhe—until at last we just had to order him to quit his nonsense. We have known Christian "workers" miss divinely presented golden opportunities of witness-bearing and soul-winning on the pious-sounding plea that before they could speak, they must "feel led". Such behaviour is a sentimental caricature of real guidance, and eventually it dissipates real spirituality. Common sense (especially *sanctified* common sense) in all such connections is one of the safest guides to our following the divine will.

So, then, to recapitulate: if we would live in the experience of continual divine guidance, there must be (1) separation from wrong ways, (2) thorough sincerity, (3) complete obedience. Also, we must not expect special guidance (a) where Scripture already directs us, (b) where duty is plain, (c) where sanctified common sense is sufficient. These rules are not hard either to remember or to practice; but they can save us from many pitfalls, and ensure glad experience of real guidance.

Listen again to the saintly George Müller. With him, the first rule in seeking guidance was as follows: "I seek at the beginning to get my heart into such a state that it has no will of its own in regard to a given matter. Nine-tenths of the trouble with people is just here. Nine-tenths of the difficulties are overcome when our hearts are ready to do the Lord's will, whatever it be. When one is truly in this state, it is usually but a little way to the knowledge of what His will is."

Sudden Attacks of Doubt

It may be wise, here, to give a word of counsel concerning sudden attacks of doubt. When guidance has become clear beyond further uncertainty, act accordingly; and decide in advance that from then onwards you will not doubt the given guidance even if things happen which seem to contradict it. Divine guidance does not render Satan inactive. It certainly puts him at a disadvantage; but if there is anyone the enemy loves to trick, it is the Christian who is really walking in the will of God and following God-given guidance. So, watch against enemy contrivances to disturb your quiet assurance in the Lord's leading. During my training for the Christian ministry, at Spurgeon's Theological College, London, England, I often used to preach at a small village-town (as it was then) named Billericay, a short train ride north of London. At that time there lived in Billericay a medical man with whom I became very friendly. He was Dr. William Shackleton, a nephew of the famous arctic explorer, Sir William Shackleton. Although not so famous as his explorer uncle, it could truly be said of him that like John the Baptist he was "great in the sight of the Lord". He and his wife had a long and outstanding record of missionary service in China.

On one occasion he told me about his call to the overseas mission field. If I remember rightly, he was the youngest student ever to graduate M.A. from the Dublin University, and one of the youngest ever to qualify as M.D. Not only was he a brilliant student, he came of a well-to-do family. Fond hopes were centred in him, and he was expected to "make a name" for himself. However, young William "got converted", and that changed his whole outlook. Later, to the dismay or anger of his family and other relatives, he had the "call" to be a missionary in China. To his worldly-wise kith and kin this was wasting wonderful talents and throwing his life away. Every argument was used to 'dissuade him. However, heart-breaking though it was to young William, even the alienation of his nearest and dearest could not shake his conviction of a divine call to the mission field.

Eventually the day of sailing came. Young William stood aboard the vessel in Dublin docks. All the other departing passengers had relatives or friends bidding them goodbye, and waving from the quay-side. William was utterly alone. Not one of his angered relatives would even see him off. Amid the drizzling rain, beneath a cold, grey sky, William's feelings were such as only those know who have gone through that kind of experience. A loud blast from the ship's horn indicated that in another minute or two the vessel would loose her moorings and be away. Then, just one minute before the gang-way was lifted, William's Sunday School teacher came hurrying aboard. Almost too breathless to speak, he explained that he had been strangely hindered from getting to the dock. He had asked God to give him a message for William—and there it was, quickly scribbled on a leaf from his notebook. The brief, affectionate farewell was like a lovely sun-shaft. William thanked him, and quickly put the scribbled note inside his pocket New Testament.

After some weeks at sea William eventually reached China. When the vessel had anchored, the passengers were taken ashore in sampans, and soon, now, young William got a close-up look at the men working at the docks. Suddenly he found himself plunged into one of those deep, inward ordeals which knock one sick with a feeling of indescribable desolation. It was the sight of those Chinese dock-workers! Those sweating, emaciated-looking bodies! But most of all—those *faces*! those *faces*! He had never expected anything quite like this. He had come out all this way with a heart of compassion (as he believed) toward these people who did not know the Gospel; but now, as he looked at those *faces*, he felt utter revulsion and a nameless fear. He could never stay among those *faces*! In sudden agony he groaned, "O God, have I mis-read Thy guidance? Please give me some direct word from Thyself." He quickly pulled out his pocket New Testament —which he had not used during the voyage, because he had his study Bible with him. As he now opened his pocket Testament, out fell the note hurriedly given him at Dublin by his Sunday School teacher. It simply quoted Jeremiah 1: 8, *"BE NOT AFRAID OF THEIR FACES"*!

Others of us have had like experiences, not s'o vivid, perhaps, but just as real. The enemy will suddenly try to disturb, or even destroy, our assurance of guidance from above. Did ever a man have clearer guidance than William Carey as he set sail for India, thus becoming the progenitor of a great new missionary era? Yet did ever a God-guided man encounter more dismaying setbacks? Some of those reverses, like the burning of his precious printing machines, made it look as if even God was mocking him. Yet the grand little man never doubted the guidance which had been given him. The result was that despite tears and heartaches all permitted oppositions became overruled to still bigger conquest, to a new sense of partnership with Christ, and to the rich development of Carey's character. Never should we envy those who have no setbacks, no cause to wonder why, no strugglings in prayer because of permitted discouragements. What a lot they miss! Just as truly as God delights to *guide* His yielded servants, He loves to *tutor* them for high destiny in the yet-to-be. So, once we are clear as to guidance, let us not afterward doubt it because of seeming contradictions.

Beware of Deflection

Another counsel worth adding here is: When guidance has become clear, beware of being *deflected* from it by any seemingly spiritual advice of other Christians, however godly they may be. Away back in the First Book of Kings, chapter 13, there is an incident related about a certain prophet, "a man of God out of Judah", whom God sent to rebuke and warn the apostate king Jeroboam, first king of the break-away ten-tribed kingdom of Israel. The man of God delivered his stern message. Then, on being invited to the royal house for refreshment (for the wicked king recognised that the prophet was indeed a "man of God") he replied, "If thou wilt give me half thine house, I will not go with thee, neither will I eat bread nor drink water in this place. For so it was charged me by the word of Jehovah, saying, Eat no bread, nor drink water, nor turn again by the same way that thou camest." So he had been given unmistakably clear guidance, and he knew it. However, there dwelt "an old prophet" in Bethel, who, on hearing this, went out and intercepted him, saying, "I am a prophet also, as thou art, and an angel spake to me by the word of Jehovah: Bring him back with thee into thine house, that he may eat bread and drink water." Whereupon, accepting this advice, the man of God from Judah gave way, and side-stepped the original word of guidance from God to him. Thus the faithful messenger who could withstand a king was misled into error and disobedience by another "man of God" who gave him *fictitious* guidance, and caused his tragic death. Shakespeare's lines come to mind—

> "Oh, what authority and show of truth
> Can cunning sin cover itself withal!"

Guidance a "Second Sense"

Finally, it is encouraging to realise that hearts which are prayerfully yielded to God develop an *aptitude* to be guided. Just as in many natural arts and skills "practice makes perfect", so, in this matter of being divinely directed, by continuous receiving and honouring of such guidance we may develop a guidance *proneness*, a receptivity to it which is a kind of "second sense" Years ago, the remarkable James Vaughan of Brighton wrote some words which are just as true now as they were then. "There are thousands of points in our journey which require almost instantaneous decision as to what we ought to do. The juncture, perhaps, is such that it gives very little time to go to some friend, or even to the divine oracles of truth, or even to ponder the matter in our own mind. At such moments, a rapid perception of the right way to go is an inestimable gift. Now those who have been familiar with holy things attain, gradually, to a surprising *initiation* of what is the mind and will of God on any such matter. It is a kind of second spiritual sense. We can scarcely explain the process, but the conclusion it brings them is usually the true one, and is often far better than any outward weighing or longer thought would have given them. . . . Their first thoughts are better than second thoughts, because in their first thoughts there is less of the merely human, and more of the divine Spirit. And *who* are those whose first thoughts are thus to be depended upon? Those who, by continual and lingering intercourse with God, the Fountain of wisdom, so see an object from His point of view, and so measure it by His standard, and so feel His affections, that they can say with Paul, 'We have the mind of Christ'."

That is the *highest* kind of guidance. We shall say more about it later, but we emphasize here the *reality* of it. In reply to the question which heads this chapter: How does guidance come? we may honestly say that to the truly "spiritual mind", as above described, it comes unimpededly, luminously, almost intuitively, and continuously. Yes, thank God, it really *does*.

HOW DO WE KNOW GUIDANCE?

"Thy Word is a lamp unto my feet, and a light unto my path."—*Psalm 119: 105.*

"To the Law and to the Testimony! If they speak not according to this Word, it is because there is no light in them."—*Isaiah 8: 20.*

"Then shall we know, if we follow on to know the Lord."—*Hosea 6: 3.*

"If any man willeth to do His [God's] will, he shall know of the doctrine, whether it be of God."—*John 7: 17.*

3

HOW DO WE KNOW GUIDANCE?

How may we *recognize* divine guidance when it comes? How may we distinguish it from the merely seeming? That is an important question. In reality, however, the criteria of true guidance are easily perceivable. To begin with, here are three detector-tests of the false.

First, true guidance is *never contrary to Scripture*. If any seemingly expedient course of action contradicts any clear teaching of the written Word, then it is branded thereby as wrong. The Holy Spirit in the *child* of God never contradicts Himself in the *Word* of God.

Second, true guidance is *never contrary to plain duty*. If a seemingly guided procedure evades moral obligation, or violates honest principle, then it is spurious guidance. The Holy Spirit never contradicts the believer's conscience.

Third, true guidance is *never contrary to highest reason*. When the pressure to do something is impatient, impetuous, flurrying, or urges sudden or risky action without due reflection, it is counterfeit. Although divine guidance may sometimes *transcend* santified human intelligence, it never *collides* with it.

But now, how may we recognise *true* guidance? Well, in this connection it is instructive to review divine methods of guidance in times past. In the camp of Israel guidance was threefold:

1. The pillar of cloud and fire (Exod. 13: 21, Neh. 9: 19).
2. The blowing of the trumpets (Num. 10: 1–9).
3. The use of Urim and Thummin (Exod. 28: 30, Lev. 8: 8, etc.).

The first was guidance to the *eye*. The second was guidance to the *ear*. The third was exceptional guidance for particular episodes. The first two were outward and general; the third was inner and special.

Later, when the covenant people were settled in the land, guidance for them seems again to have been threefold.

1. The Mosaic Scripture,
2. The judge or prophet,
3. The Urim and Thummin.

The first of these was, again, guidance through the *eye* to the mind. The second was guidance through the *ear* to the mind. The third was still available, though less needed now that there was written guidance through the Scripture, and vocal guidance through the prophet.

When we come to the New Testament, this matter of guidance takes a new turn. The emphasis shifts to guidance for the *individual* rather than for a covenant people as a whole. Even in Old Testament times there certainly was guidance for the godly individual, through the written Law or by consultation with an authentic prophet, as various passages indicate; but now, in the New Testament, and with the coming of the Holy Spirit at Pentecost, the emphasis is upon individual guidance.

Moreover, in the New Testament the *instruments* of guidance change. No more the pillar or trumpets, the Urim and Thummin, the judge or seer, nor only "the Law, the Prophets, and the Writings". There are now the new teachings of Jesus, also the new and divinely inspired Scriptures of the Church; and all these are illumined by the Holy Spirit in each individual Christian believer. The individual believer himself, herself, is "led" by the indwelling Spirit! The New Testament teaching on this guidance moves in three stages. We see it—

1. In *promise*—the Gospels
2. In *experience*—the Acts
3. In *doctrine*—the Epistles

With this data now before us, it is not difficult to abstract a reliable "theory and practice" of guidance. Here it is: divine guidance comes by (1) the written Word of God, (2) the inward urge of the Spirit, (3) indication by outward circumstance. These three are not only the *means* of divine guidance; they are the *tests* of it. When these three all agree, then guidance is clear. When they do *not* all agree, we should hesitate and wait for more light. It is not necessary that all three should always occur together. Any one of them, or two of them without the third, can be guidance. But without the coincidence of all three, the other should be definite beyond need of confirmation.

So, then, we may sum up, thus far, in two propositions:

1. For general moral and spiritual guidance we have the teaching of the written Word; for general discretion in daily walk, the ever-indwelling Holy Spirit; for general direction of life, occupation, service, the indication of outward circumstance to consecrated common sense. All three are continually interweaving for our general inward and outward guidance.

2. When we need *super-normal* guidance for special choices, crises, problems, courses of action, then (a) if the written Word and the inner urge and the outer signs all agree, guidance is clear; and (b) if only two, or even if only one, of these should seem unmistakably emphatic, guidance *may* be just as sure, though in such cases the safeguard is that it must not contradict plain Scripture, plain duty, or plain common sense. Yes, mark it well: these are the three avenues of guidance—

1. The written Word
2. The inward urge
3. Outward pointers

There are some who would make these three into four, by dividing "inward urge" into (a) the exercise of our own reason or "higher judgment", and (b) impressions from the Holy Spirit. But, strictly speaking, the exercise of our own "higher judgment" *apart* from the inner directing of the Holy Spirit is not divine guidance. Our "higher judgment" and the urge of the Holy Spirit must be *one* if there is to be real guidance.

Many years ago, now, the saintly F. B. Meyer was returning to England from a preaching engagement in Northern Ireland. The ship crossed from Belfast to Liverpool; and the landing was at night. As the lights of Liverpool began to sparkle and twinkle away ahead, Dr. Meyer and a few others were standing on deck just near the bridge. The night was very dark. The November air was damp and chilling. The sea looked oily and evil. As the ship neared port the myriads of yellow lights along the city front and the adjoining coastline, all making shivering reflections in the greasy-looking water, did not give the homiest of welcomes to Lancashire. But it was the seeming countlessness of the lights which bothered Dr. Meyer, and he called up to the bridge, "Captain, how do you know the way to steer with that confusing mass of lights in front of you?" The captain called him to come up on the bridge. "You see, sir, it's really very simple. I'll show you how. D'you see that *big* light over to the left? And d'you see that *other* big light over there to the right of it? And now d'you see that *third* outstanding light further still this way? Well, now, keep your eyes on those three lights, and see what happens." Mr. Meyer did so. The big outer light on the left gradually moved in until it coincided with the middle one; then, as the boat slowly veered further, that light gradually merged into the third. "There, now," said the boatman, "all I have to do is to see that those three big lights become one; then I go straight forward." Even so, when the Word of Scripture, and the inward urge of the Spirit, and the corroboration of outward circumstances become one—"when those three become one," we need have no fear. We may go straight ahead. God's will is clear!

Yes, let us repeat it for emphasis, when those three all concur we may safely assume that God's will is clear. If God tells me by one of those voices to do or not to do a certain thing, He cannot tell me otherwise by another voice. If there is a contradiction in the voices, they cannot both be God's voice. It is the *harmony* of the voices which gives guidance.

Some Wise Precautions

Yet even after we have deduced our simple "theory" of divine guidance, it is well to safeguard the *practice* of it by certain wise precautions. There are many of us, perhaps, who do not need the following counsels, but there are others among us who do.

First, whether in seeking or in taking guidance from the written Word, we should *guard against fancifulness*. I have known brethren get dramatic "guidance" from texts which, by no tilt of reason, had the remotest bearing on the thing at issue. Not even the eye of a hawk could have detected the connection, but to a hyper "spiritual eye" it was just as vivid as aeroplanes now are, to some, in the first chapter of Ezekiel! What rashness and regret have been occasioned thereby! If "guidance" has to be "divined" from the Word, it is not guidance at all. I do not deny that real guidance *may* come at times by sudden impact or illumination of the Word; but the fact is, that such guidance seldom if ever comes when we are determined to find it! Moreover, when guidance *does* come that way, it always comes through texts which have a straightforward relevance, not some recondite subtlety.

Again, in receiving special guidance through the written Word, we should *guard against hurried emergency consultations*. When we are in a serious predicament it is easy to start panic-snatching at this or that or the other verse which might somehow be a wizard pointer. Not thus, however, does the Bible guide us. Those to whom it speaks most readily and reliably in emergency are those who know it familiarly through diligent, daily recourse to its pages. To such the divine Spirit can really *use* the written Word, bringing to mind just those teachings which, under His own illumination, point the way.

My own decision to train for the full-time Christian ministry was finalised in that very way. I had not wanted to be a minister, yet in my own little way I had entered into Paul's "Woe unto me if I preach not the Gospel!" I felt an inward constraint to give myself wholly to public Bible teaching. Certain circumstances, also, seemed to slant that way. Yet I was not sure. Self-aims in other directions occasioned much wrestling for a while, until I got to the place where I wanted *only* my heavenly Master's will. Then one day, as I was reading 1 Timothy 4: 11–16 (I was nineteen at the time) the completive guidance flashed into my yielded mind just when I was not particularly looking for it, and took me by surprise. So luminous and compelling did verses 15 and 16 become that I simply could not doubt their special intention for me that Friday noon hour, and I looked up at the clock to register that it was 12.50 p.m. Yes, I believe Bible guidance does come that way, again and again; but never by flurried ransacking of its pages when we are at "Wits End Corner", or by desperate grabbing after "significant" texts, like drowning men clutching at straws.

Furthermore, in seeking guidance through the written Word, we should *guard against treating it as magical*. The Bible is indeed supernatural, but it has no magic in it such as some well-meaning but credulous brethren seem to expect. There are those who pray, "Lord, guide me to a text which will speak". Then (sometimes with closed eyes) they open the Bible, or let it fall open anywhere it will, and then let the verse on which eye or finger alights be "*it*". In most cases this is not faith, but foolish presumption. Just now and again, in some sore strait, to some helplessly perplexed heart, a guidance-flash *may* come by some such random appeal to the Word; but it is the rare exception. The Bible was never meant to be treated like a Delphic Oracle; and such superstitious use of it should *never* be indulged.

I have seen some very wry faces when the Bible would not yield a magic text after several such thumbings and fingerings of its pages in supposedly devout dependence on God. I have seen, also, exasperation, resentment, anger. Only too often, also, when the Bible supposedly *has* given guidance in this way, rash action has been taken which has boomeranged back with still further trouble. Sometimes, too, this way of using the Bible occasions a rueful smile. Not long ago a lady was telling me of her trouble with insomnia. It had plagued her for months, until she was much downcast. She would lie wearily in bed, waiting in vain for sleep to come; then, by two or three o'clock a.m., she would be seized by a panicky dread that she could never get through the next day's work. One night, in considerable agitation, she sprang out of bed, exclaiming, "O God, you *must* give me some word from the Bible!" She turned on the light, and picked up her promise box. Then, with tense expectancy, sure that she would be "guided" to the right "promise", she took one out. Almost afraid of seeing what the momentous message of relief would say, she slowly unrolled the little scroll. When she saw it, weary though she was, she just had to laugh. The text was 1 Corinthians 15: 51, "*We shall not all sleep, but we shall all be changed*"! Still chuckling, she got into bed again—and dropped into pleasant slumber. (So perhaps it *was* an answer!).

Testing the "Inner Urge"

It is a precious reality that the Holy Spirit inwardly guides the prayerful Christian. This guidance is *promised* in the Gospels, by our Lord Himself: "He will guide you into all the truth" (John 16: 13). "It shall be given you in that same hour what ye shall speak; for it is not ye that speak, but the Spirit of your Father which speaketh in you" (Matt. 10: 19).

This guidance is *exhibited* in the Acts. "While Peter thought on the vision, the Spirit said unto him . . . (10: 19). "As they

ministered to the Lord, and fasted, the Holy Spirit said . . ."
(13: 2). "They assayed to go into Bithynia, but the Spirit suffered
them not" (16: 7).

This guidance is *assumed* in the Epistles, as the normal experiences of spiritual adulthood: "As many as are led by the Spirit
of God, they are the sons [Gk. *huioi,* grown sons] of God" (Rom.
8: 14). "If we live in the Spirit, let us also walk in [keep step
with] the Spirit" (Gal. 5: 25).

So, this guidance by the Holy Spirit is seen in promise, in
action, and in doctrine. It is shown to us as normal for the
Christian life, vital in Christian service, and special in the hour
of emergency. Yet, mark this well, it only operates according
to this New Testament *pattern* when we are living up to New
Testament *standards*. There are many believers who would fain
live in the continual experience of it, yet they are not prepared
to live the life of Christlike selflessness and prayerfulness which
makes it real. I believe that when we continue long enough in
honest, affectionate consecration to Christ, the Spirit's voice
within us becomes so distinct as to be easily distinguishable from
any mere autosuggestion. "My sheep *hear My voice* . . . and they
follow Me" (John 10: 27).

Perhaps many of us would do well to heed certain kindly
cautions, lest we mistake *other* voices and urges as being from the
heavenly Guide when they are not from Him at all. As we have
already said, it cannot be *His* urge if it conflicts with plain Scripture, plain duty, or consecrated common sense. Again, if it is
contrary to the guide-posts of outward circumstances, we have
ample reason to reconsider it.

The Holy Spirit's inward guidance usually comes as an urge,
or pressure; but we should ever *guard against confusing it with
mere human impression.* Many are the fanaticisms which have
orignated in a gullible yielding to uncensored inward impressions.
Many are the foolish or serious aberrations of men and move-
ments which have resulted from a fanciful following of some
bogus "inner light". Alas, it is easy enough, especially amid
disturbing circumstances, tense situations, religious excitements,
nervous apprehensiveness, to mistake vivid emotion for divine
urge, or strong autosuggestion for the voice of the Spirit. Therefore we should remember that whenever the seeming urge or
voice is excited, clamouring, pushing us to a precipitate decision

without reasonable reflection, it is *not* of the Holy Spirit. It cannot be, for it leads to what is unChristlike and altogether out of keeping with godly prayerfulness. That there *is* such a thing as "sudden" guidance by the Spirit I agree; but it never comes to the hurried and prayerless. Pentecost itself happened "suddenly", but it was after ten days of unhurried waiting on God!

Therefore, just one further word: we should *guard against any supposed "guidance" which disturbs our peace in Christ.* I call attention to a significant clause in Colossians 3: 15, "Let the peace of God rule in your hearts." The Greek word translated as "rule" is a verb form of *brabeion,* a judge or arbiter in the public games. The precise meaning of Colossians 3: 15 is, "Let the peace of God *arbitrate* in your hearts." Just as an arbiter or umpire decides in a game, giving the deciding word on any disputed point, so the indwelling "peace of God" umpires for us in this matter of guidance. When this inward peace is *disturbed* by our following some supposed guidance, then the guidance is *not* of the Holy Spirit. When we are obeying *true* guidance, one of the surest tokens is peace about it in our hearts, a peace which remains undisturbed even though there may be tumult outside us. "Be anxious about nothing," counsels Philippians 4: 6; "but in everything, by prayer and supplication, let your requests be known unto God; and the *peace of God* which passeth all understanding, shall *garrison your hearts and minds* in Christ Jesus." Yes, that is one of the sensitive but trustworthy tests of "inward urge". True guidance gives *peace*.

So, to recapitulate: the New Testament vouchsafes guidance for the Christian believer—(1) in promise—the Gospels, (2) in practice—the Acts, (3) in precept—the Epistles. The three main means of guidance are (1) the written Word, (2) the inward urge, (3) the convergence of circumstances. In taking guidance from the Scripture we should guard against (1) fancifulness, (2) hurried reaching for texts, (3) treating the written Word as magical. So far as inward urge is concerned, we should guard against confusing it with sudden ideas or impulses due to emotional tenseness, and distrust it if it occasions disturbance of our peace in Christ. To guard ourselves against imitation guidance is not at all as difficult as it may seem on paper. Often, to write about a matter like this makes it sound more complicated than in fact it is. Yet it is wise, none the less, to light these red lamps of warning, for gratuitous autosuggestion has tricked many. To the really sincere and prayerful suppliant for divine guidance, the firm pathway through these side-snares soon becomes clear. In ways better "felt" than "tell't" (as they say in Scotland) when true guidance from God comes, we *know* it.

Some Basic Ideas

It is most of all helpful to keep certain basic but easily over-looked ideas about divine guidance well in mind. The first of these is: Seek to know the will of God not just in order to be *guided*, but in order to be *used*. Most of us, if we are not careful, regard the living of the Christian life solely in its perpendicular aspect— as a straight line upwards between ourselves and God. But in reality it is *triangular*—with God as the high vertex, and the two base angles ourselves and *other people*. Our experience of God is inextricably bound up with our earthly, human relationships; so is *guidance*. Often the difficulty in getting guidance may be due to a short circuit between the two base angles of the triangle, i.e., wrong relationship between ourselves and other human beings who are just as dear to God as *we* are. The fact is, God wants so to guide us as to *use* us to the spiritual good of other persons, not merely to gratify our own hearts. Therefore guidance is hindered, and sometimes blocked, if we are not right with other people. Egocentricity has ruined many a Christian's prayer-life; and any kind of selfism which wants guidance only for self-benefit lacks the fuller and higher reasons why God should give it.

Next, since the highest purpose of guidance is to enable us to fulfil *God's* will, rather than bend His will to our own, we should practice *listening* rather than always asking. God is far more concerned to have our receptivity than our explanations. He understands our needs and circumstances too well to need our persuasions. The thing of paramount importance is our *conductivity,* and this develops in us through yieldedness and listening. In order to "listen" we do not have to make the mind a vacuum, but we *do* need to get inwardly quiet enough to hear. "Speak, Lord, for Thy servant *heareth*" said godly young Samuel. Many of us keep reversing the order and saying, "Hear, Lord, for Thy servant *speaketh*." There is a place for both; but most of us are needing to learn in the school of *hearing*.

Again: Do not stop at seeking to know God's will; get to know *God*. It has often been said that God speaks to man in six ways: (1) in Nature, or the physical creation, (2) through human conscience, (3) through the Ten Commandments and the moral Law, (4) through human history, (5) in and through the Holy Scriptures, (6) supremely through the teaching and example and death and resurrection of Christ. But since the coming of the Holy Spirit at Pentecost there is a seventh and most wonderful way of divine communication to the born-again. Not just in a theoretic way, but in deepest, inward reality most of us are needing to learn that God verily speaks *directly* to the human consciousness—Spirit to spirit. Since the Holy Spirit came, God no longer needs to appear in some visible form, as He did in Old Testament times ; and we need not envy those Old Testament worthies who needed such corporeal approaches. If only we would linger long enough and regularly enough in secret prayer, we would find God speaking directly to us "as a man speaketh to his friend" (Exod. 33: 11). That is high-level guidance!

Finally, avoid seeking divine guidance only when it seems unusually necessary. Often, with most of us, our deepest need of such guidance is when we least seem to need it ; when everything seems to be going right. So God permits recurrent tight-corner "situations" to startle or trouble or frighten or hem us in, until we sink to our knees with anxious pleadings for guidance what to do.

Far too many of us think that guidance is required only for the bigger matters—our career, wedlock, big business decisions, but scarcely for the small things of everyday life. Who are *we*, to decide which matter is "little" and which is "big"? If we could see things as God sees them we would see that many of those which we consider relatively insignificant are of pivotal or far-reaching importance. For instance, one night, years ago, in Princeton, a student phoned an undergraduate at his club and invited him round for a chat. He did so rather casually, yet with a feeling there might be guidance in it. It seemed a very small thing; but in that "chat" the undergraduate was won for Christ. Then, some time later, that new convert won *his* first convert—a girl, who became the wife of the older student in a partnership of service which has brought thousands to Christ! How often the "big" is wrapped up in the "little"! Remember: God views things qualitatively, not merely quantitatively; not in their material bulk but in their mental and moral and spiritual values—in the infinitely precious stuff of personal intelligence and character. Human destiny, even beyond the grave, may be subtly involved in happenings or circumstances which to ourselves appear almost trivial.

Therefore, our ideal should be, not only to have guidance in crises, but to live continually guided *lives*.

Remember: if divine guidance is true at all (which it provenly is) then it *must* be particular, even down to so-called details, and not merely general or "providential". It is good to find the clear-brained John Wesley insisting on this. He says:

"I do not say His *general* providence; for this I take to be a sounding word, which means just nothing. And if there be a *particular* providence, it must extend to all persons and all things. So our Lord understood it, or He could never have said, 'Even the hairs of your head are all numbered'."

As big doors swing on little hinges, so the biggest experiences of life often develop from the smallest-seeming happenings. Nearly every big discovery or invention in history has somewhere hung on a detail.

Yet we must not confuse this particularity of divine guidance with a fatalistic concept of divine *predestination* such as one sometimes finds in hyper-Calvinist quarters. Only recently we were in the company of certain ministers who, as champions of the divine sovereignty, insisted that every flap of every bird's wings, every quiver of every blade of grass in every evening breeze, every accident on the roads, every detail of human life, was rigidly forefixed in the inexorable decrees of the divine sovereignty! Such a view of the world and of human history, of course, not only makes life a vast prison, it utterly excludes any such concept as that of *guidance*; for guidance necessarily implies human *freedom*. If everything is immutably forefixed, I do not *need* guidance. Even if I *ask* for guidance, my very asking for it has been predetermined and dated! Such a theology is stifling. Thank God for the fresh air and mountain spaciousness of the Scriptures—away from those cramped, dark tunnels of such theological aberration! Man is responsibly free; his very freedom is the expression of a divine sovereignty in which God purposes to deal with earnest, loving human hearts as a gracious father deals with his children.

This prompts a yet further reflection. We must not drag down this particularity of divine guidance into the *nonsensical*: which pair of socks we are to put on; which handbag we are to carry; and the like. We almost feel like apologizing for even mentioning such an idea; but some dear people do get strange ideas! As we have said earlier, divine guidance is never wasted where it is needless. Human freedom, sense and discretion have natural play in all such incidentals. Divine guidance *does* extend to details whereever there is any moral or spiritual or other serious personal issue involved.

How do we recognise the difference between direct guidance and *conscience*? Very often the two concur. Often conscience alone is not enough. Direct guidance from God will never contradict the conscience of a sincere, prayerful, Christian believer, but it often needs to tell conscience which way to act. A little nine-year-old girl told her mother, one day that God had "guided" her about something. Her mother replied, "I think what you mean, dear, is that *conscience* told you." "No, Mom," the little girl explained; "conscience tells you the difference between right and wrong; but guidance tells you which of the *right* things you ought to do."

What about the difference between direct guidance and *reason*? It is the difference between a wonderful but limited human faculty and divine omniscience. Guidance never supplants reason but often operates *through* it. The fallibility of even the best human reason arises from three delimitations: (1) it can never be absolutely sure that it has *all* the facts; (2) it·can never be absolutely sure that it perfectly *interprets* all the facts; (3) it cannot ever be absolutely sure what the *consequences* will be after any decided course of action. In contrast, God knows all the facts, all the meanings, and all the results. Therefore, guidance requires, not that human reason should be suspended, but that it should be surrendered. There is a place for human reason to do all it can with the available data, and to evaluate as best it can all the circumstances in any given "situation". But then it must hand itself and all its reasonings over to God, for *His* direction and disposition of the matter.

How, then, do we know when this higher direction operates through reason? Samuel Shoemaker has a virile reply.

"*Guidance always comes with an authority all its own.* This varies in intensity; for guidance is sometimes the motion of a consecrated human mind mobilized to do the will of God; and sometimes it is the clear shooting-in of God's thought above our thought, transcending human thought supernaturally. I cannot wholly describe to you the experience if you have not had it, but I caution you not to make too much of a mystery or a fetish of it. Consider that an Infinite God is trying to compress His thought into terms which we can understand. You do a smiliar thing when you try to explain something to your child whose vocabulary consists only of a few nouns. You are not discouraged if he does not get it all at once: but you are available whenever he will make a further try. Most unbelief as to guidance is based on little or no experience of it."

Perhaps an extended observation on that may be *a propos* here. I am aware that to some minds these studies in guidedness (especially part one on the mechanics of it) could seem too definite to be modern, even riskily superficial in their confidence that when conditions are really fulfilled, guidance certainly comes. So let it be realized: what we are saying is said knowingly in face of that. We have met those who mourn, "I *did* fulfil the conditions, but guidance never came"; and those who aver, "Many human experiences are beyond the operation of guidance according to set rules." We too have known dismay amid quandary and the apparent unconcern of a silent heaven.

We sympathize with those who deem that any idea of guidance which ties it to the apron-strings of set regulations is rather naive. Yet we are persuaded they are wrong; that they too dimly perceive the deeper meanings of communion with God. Valid experience gives ample proofs that we *can* be "definite". Of course, it is the fashion now to be indefinite on such matters. Indefiniteness is often regarded as the superior cautiousness of scholarship. It can also be, however, the foot-dragging of educated unbelief. We have watched its operation in certain brilliantly intellectual acquaintances, and have seen it gradually atrophy faith. With clear Scripture before us, I believe that we *may* be definite about divine guidance. I also believe that most obscurities are *somewhere* due to unsuspected default in ourselves. Reflect what a superlative wonder it is to be God-guided. Then reflect again what loving, utter commitment to God it *must* demand. At times, when I myself have seemed to be denied guidance, I have later descried lurkings of selfism still unexpelled.

Another lesson many of us learn too slowly is, that guidance is not meant only for "situations" which compel us to seek it. It is those who live guided *lives* who best know guidance in "situations". Let those with hesitations ponder that well. There is a high *life*-level of fellowship with God on which guidance is no longer a hazy puzzle, but a shining reality. It will not occur to those who mistake indefiniteness for sagacity that they *could* be wrong; but it is a fact that doubt as to guidance often stems from a blend of *natural* maturity with spiritual *im*maturity. Having been Christians for years, it is easy for us to think that because we have matured naturally we have equally matured spiritually. We readily mis-read ourselves. Indeed, what we compliment in ourselves as seasoned cautiousness *may* be spiritual poor-sightedness; and we may be seeing only shadows where the truly developed spiritual mind sees luminous realities. There is a world of meaning in Genesis 24: 27, "*I, being in the way, the Lord led me.*" If only we *lived* in "the way" of guidance, how often our sigh, "All these things are against me" (Gen. 42: 36) would soar into the song, "All things work together for good" (Rom. 8: 28)!

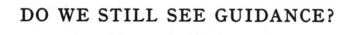

DO WE STILL SEE GUIDANCE?

.

Most men today seem to regard God as distant and silent. When pressed for an expression of faith, they will admit they believe in the existence of God, but they do not anticipate any message from Him. . . . Yet God is alive and active: He speaks today. Our problem is that we simply are not listening. We are like the silly king in Bernard Shaw's play, *Saint Joan*. When the young girl heard God speaking to her, and told the king about the voices, he was angry. "I am the king," he thundered. "Why don't the voices come to me?" To which Joan answers sweetly, "Because you are not listening".

Dr. W. Goddard Sherman.

"Having eyes, see ye not? and having ears, hear ye not?"

Mark 8: 18.

4

DO WE STILL SEE GUIDANCE?

So far, we have asked three questions about divine guidance: (1) Why do we need it? (2) When do we get it? (3) How do we know it? The next question, in logical order, is: *Do we still see it?* Is it still operative and verifiable in these days of crowded urbanization, complexity of civilisation, and other modern developments which submerge the individual in the mass? Is it still recognizable and demonstrable despite the fashionable idea that "natural law" leaves no place for *super*natural guidance?

Well, perhaps the most reassuring answer is to give a few illustrations from living experience. I have known some of the most obstinate anti-supernaturalists won over to the Christian faith through the impressive evidence of divine guidance in the lives of Christian believers. Some of those sceptics had been students of philosophy and psychology, and were pretty well "brain-washed" in the modern distrust of subjective experience. They could (at least to their own satisfaction) scientifically analyse away any such "experience". Yet now those same persons are convinced believers, knowing that they are dealing with a reality which simply cannot be satisfactorily accounted for by purely natural or human forces. That which argument could never prove to them, experience has *demonstrated*.

Most of the examples which I here give are from friends whom I myself have met; so they are "first hand". I do not say that they are of an exciting kind, though there may be touches here and there of what we call *"extra*ordinary" guidance; but they surely do indicate, and at the same time illustrate, divine guidance in the life of the Christian individual. The first of them links yesterday with today.

When the Wrong Road is Right

When we were in Los Gatos, California, recently, we came across one of the dearest old saints we have ever met, a retired minister of the Gospel, full of mature godliness and ripe good humour and wistful reminiscences. Among many unforgettable anecdotes which he related to us concerning his early days was the following. On one occasion, away back in the quiet old horse-and-buggy America, when he himself was a young minister still in his twenties, he was itinerating on horse-back in a sparsely populated area of Texas and came to a place where two roads forked off in different directions. In those days, in those places, it was a serious thing to get on the wrong road, but there was no road-sign, so he could only guess as to which road he should take. He saw that one of the two seemed more used than the other, and that it also seemed to stretch in the desired direction. So that was the road he took. However, after riding from mid-morning until well on in the afternoon he was suddenly disappointed to find that the road ended at a river, right there in the heart of the country, "miles from anywhere". There was no road *beyond* the river, and no road along *beside* the river. The road he had travelled just stopped —and so did he! It seemed all the more dismaying because he had specially prayed that God would guide him, and now it appeared as though guidance had broken down.

However, as he glanced around, he saw an elderly-looking man chopping some wood, so he dismounted and went over to enquire how best he could get on a road to such-and-such a town. The man said, "Mister, there ain't no road to there from here. You'll have to go back to that fork in the road again." But as soon as the wood-chopper learned that the wanderer was a Baptist minister he said, "Preacher, you ain't going back to that fork-road at all. Just you call and knock at our house over there, and tell my Missus that you's a Baptist minister. She'll no let you leave here. She's prayed for years that a Baptist preacher would come out here." Our friend explained, however, that he could not possibly stay, as he had a booking in the town he was making for; but he promised at least to knock at the door of the woodman's house and greet the lady there.

She was an earnest-faced woman; and the moment she knew that the stranger was a Baptist preacher her eyes lit up. "Sir," she firmly declared, "you are not going on to that town; you are staying right here." Although he protested that he simply must move on because people were waiting, she would have none of it. "You couldn't get there tonight, anyhow," she said. "Come in, and make yourself at home. Nobody could be more welcome." Tears came into her eyes, as she added, "You're the answer to my prayers of twenty years, that God would send a preacher to this place. We'll have a meeting for you tonight."

She was as good as her word. She scoured the locality and gathered the folk in. The little hall was packed. The people were intent. The power of the Lord was on the preacher, and he knew it. He made an appeal; a number responded. The dear woman who had convened the meeting was sitting next to her two daughters and her son, Della, Mollie, and Fred. The father, too, was sitting in the same row. The mother started pleading with Della; and out came Della to the front of the hall, to kneel with the others who had come to the Saviour's feet. Then Mollie came; then Fred. They were truly saved, and showed it through tears of joy. Meanwhile the father had slipped out of the hall, complaining, "It's getting too stuffy in there"; but mother and children pursued him, and brought him in again, entreating him to receive the Saviour. Soon after, he too was on his knees, seeking and finding salvation. The whole family was now united and rejoicing in Christ. Oh, it was a wonderful meeting! It kept on for several days! Apparently every unconverted person around there was won to the Saviour!

And *now* the preacher *knew* why he had been allowed to take that wrong road! Guidance had not broken down at all. It had been a higher kind of guidance than he himself had suspected. He could only keep on saying, "This is the Lord's doing; it is marvellous in our eyes" (Ps. 118: 23). As Samson made up a riddle about the lion, so the rejoicing young preacher found himself coining a riddle of the road. Question: "When is the wrong road the right road?" Answer: "When *God* sends you on it." The young preacher had prayed for guidance, and God had truly given it; not quite after the pattern that the human servant had expected, but according to Isaiah 55: 9, "As the heavens are higher than the earth, so are My ways higher than your ways, and My thoughts than your thoughts."

The foregoing reminiscence illustrates the fact that divine guidance sometimes comes in least expected ways, and is often bigger than our asking. Monica prayed that her clever son might not go to the big city with its seductive temptations. Yet he was permitted to go. So, then, was her prayer ignored? No: in the city her son heard the preaching of the Gospel and became saved! Succeeding centuries have known him as "Saint Augustine". The answer was bigger than the prayer. So, often, is the answer to our prayer for guidance, if we are truly walking with our Lord.

Deadline—Two o' clock

One morning, while a minister friend of mine was busy in his study, his mind was suddenly gripped by a strong conviction that he should visit a certain jail, to see a man who was under death sentence for murder. He did not know the condemned man, but he knew the circumstances of the crime. The condemned man had been a decent-living fellow, and, apparently, comfortably married, except that his mother-in-law was bent on persuading his wife to start having a drink with her at a local "pub"—which indeed she eventually succeeded in doing. From that first, fateful glass, the young wife began to slip into trouble. As her drinks became more frequent, she allowed some philanderer in the "pub" to make advances to her, and a wrong relationship developed. This was brought to the notice of her husband, who waylaid the other man with intent to thrash him. Instead, he murdered him.

When the strong urge seized my friend, to see this condemned man, he scarce knew what to do. He had much work on hand. The jail was a train journey away. Even if he went there, would he be allowed to see the man? Besides, what good could it do now? Yet he had been praying, earlier, that the day might be guided, and he was convinced now that the strange urge was from the Holy Spirit. He looked up the railway time-table, found a suitable train, and decided to go. As "the stars in their courses fought against Sisera", so it seemed as though everything was set on preventing his getting that train, but he got it "in the nick of time", and eventually reached the prison. After the usual formalities he was admitted, but then there was delay due to hesitation by the prison authorities. Finally, he was given permission to see the condemned man. At the cell a small grating was opened, and he stood face to face with the prisoner. He began quickly to explain the seemingly strange reason for his coming, and how he would have arrived earlier but for delays. Just then, the boom of the prison clock reverberated through the corridor as it slowly struck *two o' clock in the afternoon*. As the sound died away, the prisoner suddenly burst into convulsive sobbing. Then, struggling to control himself, he groaned out the words, "I never meant to kill . . . but . . . I am to die. . . . This morning, in my agony, I cried, 'O God, if you really exist, and if you really hear, and if you care, please, oh, please, let me know in *some* way . . . and, oh, God, I give you until two o'clock this afternoon'!" When my friend left the prison a bit later, the young man in that cell had truly found the glad assurance of eternal salvation in Christ; and my friend went home gratefully musing on the wonderful guidance which had contrived his arrival at that prison cell *just as the prison clock boomed out two o'clock*!

I readily agree that incidents of such dramatic guidance are not of too common occurrence. The foregoing episode is submitted not to illustrate the usual *way* of guidance, but to underline the *fact* of it in the individual Christian life.

A Two-hour Delay

Some years ago, the late Bishop Taylor Smith was travelling by railway from somewhere in northern England to somewhere south. He missed the connection at Leeds, Yorkshire, and found he had two hours to wait. As always, in such circumstances, he accepted this as "permissive providence", and prayed for guidance, if God had some special purpose in allowing the delay. Strolling from the station to the big Square outside, he sat on a form, and noticed that its only other occupant was a middle-aged man who looked the very picture of misery. Shabbily dressed, bent shoulders, head drooped down on his hands, he took no notice whatever of the burly clergyman who now sat near him. Still counting on guidance, the bishop said, "You seem to be in some deep trouble." "Yes, I sure am," the man muttered, without lifting his eyes. "I'm at the end of things, mister." He coughed hoarsely, then added, "Maybe you'll no believe me, mister, but tonight I'm going to end everything; and I'm just having this last sit out here." "But is there *no* one can help you?" asked the bishop. "Nobody," came the dejected reply. Then, after a pause, head sagging still lower, the man added, "Beggin' your pardon, stranger, there's *just one* man who could have helped me, if I could have found him; but I havna' seen him these fifteen years, and I've no notion where he is." "Who is he?" asked the bishop. "He was my army padre in France during the War, but I clean forget his name." "Which regiment and company were you in?— and what battles were you in?" enquired the bishop. The man slowly told him, still without looking up. Then, stretching out his hand, and gently lifting the man's head up, the bishop said, "Well, my brother, look at me; your man is right here; *I* was that padre; and after all these years God has sent me to help you here and now!"

Would anyone stubbornly pretend that such prayer-atmo-sphered transpirings are mere coincidence? They are the opera-tion of real divine guidance in and through consecrated indi-viduals. And what channels of blessing we become when we are living such guided lives!

Instances of a like sort could be compiled in bookfuls, but un-fortunately the narrating of them runs away with more space than we can spare. All we can do is to add a few more, mostly of a briefer sort.

The Right Target

My beloved mother was out delivering Gospel tracts in a slummy city area. She prayed that each tract might find the right target. She knocked at a door, and waited. No one answered, but she heard movement within, so she knocked again. After three knocks and waits the door slowly opened, and a rough-faced man was there, on hands and knees, or, rather, on hands and stumps —for both legs had been amputated above the knees, as a result of a recent accident. My mother immediately apologised for having brought him to the door, but he did not mind, and was willing enough to take the tract. He gave one glance at it, and then, with quivering lips, asked, "Missis, did you pick this one specially for *me*?" The title of the tract was: *"NOT A LEG TO STAND UPON!"*—and it was used of God to bring home to the man his *spiritual* condition before God.

A Change of Pew

One Sunday morning, just as my dear wife was entering her usual pew at church, she became strangely but irresistibly con-strained to change place and sit near the front, with a certain lady who at that time was beset by sore trial. Momentarily she hesitated lest her unusual action should give a wrong impression to those around, or cause embarrassment to the lady herself. Yet along with the surprise urge came a peaceful assurance that it was of the Spirit; so she acted accordingly. It was not until eight or nine months later that she learned what this bit of obeyed guidance had meant. The saintly woman with whom my dear wife went to sit had been struggling with the problem as to whether she should still come to church, owing to the ugly scandal now associated with the family name. She was scared of curious looks and questions. She had pleaded, "Dear Lord, guide me. Preserve me from unwise enquirers; and, if it please Thee, give me a sign: *may Mrs. Baxter be led to come and sit with me.*" This, by the way, is an instance in which guidance prayed for by *one* person was answered through guidance given to *another*.

Pastorate Guidance

A young minister, on leaving seminary, declined several invitations to thriving churches because he felt guided to a seemingly "ne'er do well" church in the English midlands. After several years there, with gracious sealings of the Holy Spirit on the small but growing work, enquiry showed that only at big cost could the premises be suitably adapted. This raised the question: "Am I to stay here years longer, raising that money?" A wonderful "offer" which was made for the premises at that time would have built a new church in a better area, but the members said "No". Inward conviction and outward direction blended as he now sought guidance about a new sphere. Five invitations came, one after another, to churches in London. He visited each in turn; yet although each gave a unanimous "call", the inner voice said "No".

Months passed; then came an invitation from away up north-east. Rather reluctantly he went, saying, "Who wants to live *there,* the 'edge o' beyond'?" Yet as he entered the pulpit on the Sunday morning, two impressions at once registered: (1) "What a drab place!" (2) "This is where you are coming." The Elders met after the service; *they* knew, too, just as definitely. Guidance was unmistakable.

Is that all? No. That influential church had been without pastor two years. The officebearers were cautious, and had decided that on no account should that large church have a *young* pastor. Yet strangely enough, three letters had come simultaneously, all recommending this same "young man". The first of these letters was from an outstanding minister whose urge to write had come suddenly one morning while he was shaving. The second was from a well-known Christian leader who had wakened during the night with a curious impression that he must write. The third was from a college principal who had written under similar constraint. It *looked* like guidance; but the minister whom they all named was a *young* man; so he was put right at the end of the "candidates" list, and only invited even then as a courtesy to the three writers.

Eventually an older minister from up north was at the point of being chosen. He was to preach for them once again with the almost foregone conclusion that he was "the man". The Sunday *prior* to that, the undesired *young* minister came. He was younger than *any* of their former ministers; yet at once *he* knew, and *they* knew, and *all* knew, that he was to be their next pastor. From the beginning there was blessing; and during the third year super-natural revival visited that church with very blessed effects in many hearts, and such incoming crowds that there had to be two evening services each Sunday.

Was even *that* all? No; God had overruled the ten months or so during which those well-meaning Elders had pushed the young minister's name to the end of their list. It was during those months that his five preachings in London took place. Later, when special commitments took him to London, he found the way wonderfully prepared through contacts made on those five visits!

The reason why I can relate all this with such inside detail will have become obvious by now. It was by similar clear guidance that my dear wife and I were taken to our eighteen-year ministry in Edinburgh, Scotland. It was by equally distinct evidence of higher control that we were eventually drawn away from the settled pastorate to the wider ministry of these later years. All the way through, it has been the same. When we have made sure of wanting only *God's* will, not our own, direction has come in ways which have reassured our hearts and brought thanksgivings to God.

Some of the foregoing incidents represent somewhat unusual kinds of guidance, others the less spectacular, but all of them, and scores of others which might have been given, document the *fact* of divine guidance—a true guidance which operates in the hearts and lives of all who live in prayerful yieldedness to God.

Yes, we say that the foregoing instances, along with the many more which might be furnished, substantiate the *fact* of divine guidance; for how else shall we honestly explain them? Is it fair to keep on charging the witnesses with imaginativeness, exaggera-tion, or insincerity, when in their hundreds they are mainly men and women of acknowledged sober judgment and upright char-acter? Again and again the features are such as simply cannot be accounted for on telepathic or psychological grounds. Nor is it scientifically feasible to explain them away as being merely accumulations of pure *coincidence*. Many of them are of such a nature that any attempt to dismiss them as coincidence is decidedly *un*scientific—for the following three reasons. First: they reveal *purpose,* whereas coincidence is blindly fortuitous. Second: they express *coherence,* especially those which form a *chain* of guidance, link by link, whereas mere coincidence is patternless chance. Third: they are such direct answers to prayer, in many cases, as to establish a *cause-and-effect* relation, whereas coincidence is a quite mindless turn of circumstance which cannot have *any* such connection.

A Christian friend of mine had reached the most important examination of her life, if she was to qualify as a teacher. She had prayed about the whole of her career, and the evidences of an answering guidance had seemed unmistakable. She had prayed about her choice of subjects, and again the desired direction had seemed clear. She had prayed about the optional place and date (out of several) where and when she should offer herself for the decisive test. The one big problem was the long *oral* part of the examination—for she had a chronic, nervous deafness which any tension in the examination room would aggravate, thus incapacitating her even to hear the questions, let alone answer them. This was made a matter of earnest prayer. To her dismay, when she entered the examination hall, she found herself put at the corner desk in the very back row! The platform and examiner's desk away at the front of the room seemed a mile away. There was no loud-speaker system. The examination started. Contrary to all precedent, the examiner left his desk, walked down the hall to the very back row, right to *her* desk at the corner, and gave out all his questions from there! It was just another link in a *chain* of guidance answering to a chain of *prayer.*

One of my first eye-openers in what we may call the more dramatic forms of such guidance was a reading of Charles Grandison Finney's experiences. The America of Finney's day was markedly different from now. It was mainly agricultural and much simpler. The automobile had not filled it with millions of roads and never-ending traffic. Many of the obscurer rural areas were very backward educationally, socially, and in other ways. However, without added reminders of that, let me quote one of Finney's experiences in full. Perhaps it may seem far removed from the kind of guidance which most of ourselves need, whose circumstances are so much less exciting, less public, than the famous Finney's. Most of ourselves need guidance amid prosaic, ordinary, hum-drum surroundings. Yet our *faith* in the divine directing of human lives is often strengthened by testimonies such as Finney and others have left. So, here is Finney's own account.

A Testimony From Finney

"Soon after I was licensed to preach I went into a region of country where I was an entire stranger. I went there at the request of a Female Missionary Society, located in Oneida County, New York. Early in May, I think, I visited the town of Antwerp, in the northern part of Jefferson County. I stopped at the village hotel, and there learned that there were no religious meetings held in that town at the time. They had a brick meeting-house, but it was locked up. By personal efforts I got a few people to assemble in the parlour of a Christian lady in the place, and preached to them on the evening after my arrival.

"As I passed round the village, I was shocked with the horrible profanity that I heard among the men wherever I went. I obtained leave to preach in the school-house on the next Sabbath; but before the Sabbath arrived I was much discouraged, and almost terrified, in view of the state of society which I witnessed. On Saturday the Lord applied with power to my heart the following words, addressed by the Lord Jesus to Paul, Acts 18: 9, 10: 'Be not afraid, but speak, and hold not thy peace; for I am with thee, and no man shall set on thee to hurt thee; for I have much people in this city.' This completely subdued my fears; but my heart was loaded with agony for the people.

"On the Sunday morning I arose early, and retired to a grove not far from the village to pour out my heart before God for a blessing on the labours of the day. I could not express the agony of my soul in words; but struggled, with much groaning and, I believe, with many tears, for an hour or two without getting relief. I returned to my room in the hotel; but almost immediately came back to the grove. This I did thrice. The last time I got complete relief, just as it was time to go to meeting.

"I went to the school-house, and found it filled to its utmost capacity. I took out my little pocket Bible, and read for my text: 'God so loved the world, that He gave His only begotten Son, that whosoever believeth in Him should not perish, but have everlasting life.' I exhibited the love of God in contrast with the terrible manner in which He was treated by those for whom He gave up

His Son. I charged home their profanity upon them; and, as I recognised among my hearers several whose profanity I had particularly noticed, in the fulness of my heart and the gushing of my tears, I pointed to them, and said, 'I heard these men call upon God to damn their fellows.' The Word took powerful effect. Nobody seemed offended, but almost everybody greatly melted. At the close of the service, the amiable landlord, Mr. Copeland, rose and said that he would open the meeting-house in the afternoon. He did so. The meeting-house was full, and, as in the morning, the Word took powerful effect. Thus a powerful revival commenced in the village, which soon after spread in every direction.

"I think it was on the second Sabbath after this, when I came out of the pulpit in the afternoon, an aged man approached, and said to me, 'Can you not come and preach in our neighbourhood? We have never had any religious meetings there'. I inquired the direction and the distance, and arranged to preach there the next afternoon, Monday, at five o'clock, in their school-house. I had preached three times in the village, and attended two prayer-meetings on the Lord's day; and on Monday I went on foot to fulfil this appointment. The weather was very warm that day, and before I arrived there I felt almost too faint to walk, and greatly discouraged in mind. I sat down in the shade by the wayside, and felt as if I was too faint to reach there, and if I did, too much discouraged to open my mouth to the people.

"When I arrived I found the house full, and immediately commenced the service by reading a hymn. They attempted to sing, but the horrible discord agonised me beyond expression. I leaned forward, put my elbows upon my knees and my hands over my ears, and shook my head withal, to shut out the discord, which even then I could barely endure. As soon as they had ceased to sing, I cast myself down upon my knees, almost in a state of desperation. The Lord opened the windows of Heaven upon me, and gave me great enlargement and power in prayer. Up to this moment I had had no idea what text I should use on this occasion. As I rose from my knees the Lord gave me this: 'Up, get you out of this place [Sodom], for the Lord will destroy this city.' I told the people, as nearly as I could recollect, where they would find it, and went on to tell them of the destruction of *Sodom*. I gave them an outline of the history of Abraham and Lot, and their relations to each other; of Abraham's praying for *Sodom*; and of *Lot* as the only pious man that was found in the city. While I was doing this I was struck with the fact that the people looked exceed-ing angry about me. Many countenances appeared very threaten-ing, and some of the men near me looked as if they were about to strike me. This I could not understand, as I was only giving them, with great liberty of spirit, some interesting sketches of Bible history in connection with Sodom.

"As soon as I had completed the historical sketch, I turned upon them, and said that I had understood they had never had any religious meetings in that neighbourhood; and applying that fact, I thrust at them with the sword of the Spirit with all my might. From this moment the solemnity increased with great rapidity. In a few moments there seemed to fall upon the congregation an instantaneous shock. I cannot describe the sensation that I felt, nor that which was apparent to the congregation; but the Word seemed *literally* to cut like a sword. The power from on high came down upon them in such a torrent that they fell from their seats in every direction. In less than a minute nearly the whole con-gregation were either down on their knees, or on their faces, or in *some* position prostrate before God. Everyone was crying or groaning for mercy upon his own soul. They paid no further attention to me or to my preaching. I tried to *get* their attention; but I could not. I observed the aged man who had invited me there, still retaining his seat near the centre of the house. He was *staring* around him with a look of unutterable astonishment. Pointing to him, I cried at the top of my voice: 'Can't you *pray*?' He knelt down and roared out a short prayer, about as loud as he could halloo; but they paid no attention to him. After looking round for a few moments, I knelt down and put my hand on the head of a young man who was kneeling at my feet, and engaged in prayer for mercy on his soul. I got his attention, and preached Jesus in his ear. In a few moments he seized Jesus by faith, and then broke out in prayer for those around him. I then turned to another in the same way, and with the same result; and then another, and another, till I know not how many had laid hold of Christ and were full of prayer for others.

"After continuing in this way till nearly sunset, I was obliged to commit the meeting to the charge of the old gentleman who had invited me, and go to fulfil an appointment in another place for the evening. In the afternoon of the next day I was sent for to go down to this place, as they had not been able to break up the meeting. They had been obliged to leave the school-house, to give place to the school; but had removed to a private house near by, where I found a number of persons still, too anxious and too much loaded down with conviction to go to their homes. These were soon subdued by the Word of God, and I believe all obtained a hope before they went home.

"Observe, I was a total stranger in that place, and had never seen nor heard of it until as I have related. But here, at my second visit, I learned that the place was called Sodom, by reason of its wickedness; and the old man who invited me was called Lot, because he was the only professor of religion in the place. After this manner the revival broke out in this neighbourhood.

"I have not been in that neighbourhood for many years; but in 1856, I think, while labouring in Syracuse, New York, I was introduced to a minister of Christ from the St. Lawrence County, by the name of Cross. He said to me: 'Mr. Finney, you don't know me; but do you remember preaching in a place called Sodom?' etc. I said: 'I shall never forget it.' He replied: 'I was then a young man, and was converted at that meeting.' He is still living, a pastor in one of the churches in that county, and is the father of the principal of our preparatory department. Those who have lived in that region can testify of the permanent results of that blessed revival. I can only give in words a *feeble* description of that wonderful manifestation of power from on high attending the preaching of the Word."

The foregoing incident in Finney's memoirs lit a flame of wonder in my mind when I first read it as a youth of seventeen or eighteen years old. That divine guidance should control such vivid detail with such spectacular results astonished me. Yet if I may say so, in humble, thankful testimony, many a time since then, in my own experience, and in the observed experience of other Christians, I have seen equally remarkable demonstrations of guidance in similar even though perhaps less florid circumstances. If it were becoming to do so, we could fill pages narrating episodes in which the dovetailing developments simply could not be honestly explained apart from direct divine guidance and control of detail. What if there are those who "cannot believe" (as they say)? Does that invalidate the endless chain of evidence?

None are so blind as those who will not see,
  None are so deaf as those who will not hear;
Though proofs build up like solid masonry,
  And honest logic reads the meaning clear;

Unless almighty God, with deafening shout,
　　Or flaming letters, speaks from out the skies,
Agnostic prejudice can only doubt
　　All other kinds of proof to ears and eyes:
And if God *wrote* across the skies this day
　　In flaming signs which *had* to be believed,
Tomorrow learned doubt again would say,
　　"Our very senses must have been deceived!"

Most of us who read these lines, however, are of a very different cast of mind. As we gratefully survey the many evidences of our heavenly Father's guidance we ally ourselves with F. W. H. Myer's lines,

Whoso has felt the Spirit of the Highest
　　Cannot confound, nor doubt Him, nor deny;
Yea, though, O World, with one voice thou deniest
　　Stand thou on that side; for on this am I.

MAY WE NOW HAVE GUIDANCE?

"This God is our God for ever and ever: He will be our Guide even unto death."

Psalm 48: 14.

"I am Jehovah, thy God, which teacheth thee to profit, which leadeth thee by the way that thou shouldst go."

Isaiah 48: 17.

Open my inward eyes,
Teacher divine ;
Spirit of glad surprise,
Within me shine :
Quicken my inward sight,
So that I see
Gleaming in clearest light
Thy word to me.

Open my inward ears,
Till, as I pray,
My inward being hears
All Thou wilt say :
And as I here commune,
Master so dear,
Set all my mind attune
Thy voice to hear.

Open my inmost mind
Wholly to Thee,
Deep there within to find
Thy will for me :
So may Thy perfect will
Guide this of mine,
And all my days fulfil
Thine own design.

J.S.B.

5

MAY WE NOW HAVE GUIDANCE?

OUR reflections on this subject of divine guidance evoke a further question: "May we now have it?" To this further question our gathered findings surely ring out a clear answer: "Yes . . . if . . ." The "Yes" on the divine side is firm, providing the "if" on the human side honours the straightforward conditions. Our Lord's word in John 7: 17 underlines this: "If any man will *practice* His [God's] will, he shall *know*. . . ." So, then, in this present chapter let us "wrap up" our reflections on the subject thus far.

Following the examples of divine guidance given in our preceding chapter, let us be sure that we have swept our minds clean of every subtle doubt about it. There is a remarkable little word in Amos 9: 9. The prophet is announcing the soon-coming punishment and dispersal of Israel, the "sinful kingdom". Then Jehovah Himself says through the prophet, "I will sift the house of Israel among all nations, like as corn is sifted in a sieve; yet shall not the *least grain* fall upon the earth." How tiny is a "grain"! How tinier still is "the *least* grain"! Yet amid all the chaff which is to be so widely dispersed by the wind of judgment, God does not lose sight of even one grain of the pure wheat (i.e. the truly godly soul); no, not even of "the *least* grain"!

Since then Jesus has come to tell us that not even the sparrow sold for a farthing is overlooked by the heavenly Father's all-seeing eyes. How dear each one of us is to God! Let us never doubt it. Our twentieth-century "age of science" has altered much of man's thinking about God and the universe, but (remember) it has not altered *God*! Science may have recently discovered "natural laws", but it is God who still runs them—not man. God and His behaviour in His universe are not changed. It is still true that He "paints the wayside lily" as well as "lights the evening star"; that the "hairs of our head" are numbered as well as the starry hosts; that amid the ever vaster welter of history, He "standeth in the shadows, keeping watch upon His own". The whole Bible tells us this; and Jesus wrote His signature to it in the crimson ink of Calvary. As Isaac Watts paraphrases it,

He formed the stars, those heavenly flames,
He counts their number, calls their names ;
His wisdom's vast, and knows no bound,
A deep where all our thoughts are drowned.

But saints are lovely in His sight ;
He views His children with delight ;
He sees the hopes and fears they bear,
And looks and loves His image there.

Dear Christian, once for all fling away doubt (if any remains) as to the *individualizing* love and care and guidance of God. He loves and cares for *you*, in particular. He wants to guide *you*, individually. God does not see you merely as a speck in a mass. Saved by the "precious blood" of His dear Son, and "born again" by the regenerating divine Spirit, so that from your spiritually reborn nature you intuitively cry, "Abba Father", are you not uniquely precious to Him? Fling doubt to the moles and the bats! Learn *really* to trust the loving care and guiding hand of God.

First, then, if we would experience definite and continual divine guidance, we must feel such *need* for it, and have such *desire* for it, that we resolutely exclude from our lives everything which would frustrate it. How can we reasonably expect divine guidance unless we strongly feel such need and desire? How can there be *continuing* guidance if there is only intermittent seeking of it? Why should the Holy Spirit condescend to give us even now-and-then guidance, if with careless neglect we treat Him as only an emergency Consultant? More than all else, we Christian believers should desire holiness of heart, guidedness of life, usefulness in soul-winning, and the consciousness of our Lord's indwelling.

Second, in our seeking for guidance there must be an utterly sincere *intention to obey* the divine will when it is revealed. A newspaper editor's column on a large conference of Democrats said, "Their votes were decided even before their minds were made up". In other words, not even their true convictions were allowed to change their fixed decisions. It parallels with those people who plead for supernatural guidance when already, in the deep subtleties of their nature, they have pre-decided which way to go. I have known persons keep on pleading for guidance when, by all tests, it had already come. They piously pretended that guidance had *not* yet come, because, deep down, they were re-

sentfully dodging that which was already made plain. Such re-
ligiously dressed duplicity gradually thwarts all further guidance,
until eventually the only guidance effective for such persons is
that which is described in Psalm 32: 9.

Third, we should never accept as divine guidance any course
of action contrary to Scripture, duty, and prayerful common-
sense. However tempting it may seem, if a course of action clashes
with the written Word of God, it courts disaster. Even if it is not
against the actual *wording* of Scripture, it is just as much a wrong
road if it swings away from the principles or *sense* of Scripture.
Not long ago, I heard a very decided brother laying it down that
2 Corinthians 6: 14 ("Be not unequally yoked together with unbelievers") does not refer to marriage at all, and that therefore it
is wrong for us to keep using that text against the marrying of
sincere Christians to persons who, although not "converted" in
our sense of the word, are equally sincere, and in every other way
suitable life-partners. Well, it is true that 2 Corinthians 6: 14 does
not refer by *word* to wedlock, but it does so in *principle*. The
"unequal yoke" *includes* wedlock: and to disregard it is to take a
pleasant-seeming wrong road which often leads to heart-break or
bitter regret.

Even as I write there comes to mind the matron of a large
hospital, who, just as she was beginning to think that love and
marriage would never now come her way, found that special atten-
tions were being paid to her by one of the most charming men any
woman could wish to meet. He was wealthy, well-known, and of
high repute. His avowal of love and proposal of wedlock were all
that could be desired; and her heart went out to him. But there
was the one big difficulty that *she* was a born-again Christian
believer, whereas he was not. Well-meaning friends told her that
she was being a fool not to seize her glamorous opportunity. *He*
would never stand in the way of her "religious convictions".
Almost certainly she would later win him over to "*her* way of
thinking". Eventually, she gave him her "Yes", and they were
wedded—though not without her knowing that she was contradict-
ing the Word and disregarding the inward voice of the Holy Spirit.
She had said to herself and her friends, "It's my one chance of
married happiness, and I'm going to take it". We need give no
details as to the unexpected turn of things *after* their "unequal
yoke"; but fifteen years later she wrung her hands and sobbed, "I
have not had one happy day in fifteen years!"

Three Cautions

Furthermore, in our seeking for divine guidance we do well to
heed three amber lamps of "caution": (1) The commonest *hind-
rance* is our allowing "self" to get in the way. (2) The commonest
danger is our following after mere "impressions". (3) The commonest *mistake* is our thinking that guidance comes only through
the abnormal.

Take the first of these, i.e. the obtruding of *self* into our seeking
for guidance. Some years ago, when we were making our way up
through the Himalayas to Kalimpong, we were met at Bagdogra
by a smiling Assamese friend who insisted on photographing us.
The day was brilliantly sunny. Our photographer stepped back
from us a pace or two, then, standing between us and the sun,
clicked his snapshot. The result was that when the picture came
out his own shadow was right across it, obscuring our faces. By
parallel, that is always what happens when "self" obtrudes into
our praying for divine direction: it obscures our Lord's face,
making guidance indistinct. When we seek heavenly leading there
must be a thorough subduement of our own plans and preferences
and purposes. We must cease from self-wisdom, self-seeking, self-
choosing. This does not mean a suspension of our normal mental
activities, such as reason and reflection, but it does mean a sub-
ordination of them. It does not mean that the mind must become
a vacuum (for that invites *false* guidance), but it does mean that
the mind must be evacuated of all secret thought to get divine
guidance for self-advantage. The more completely we can get
"self" out of the way, and the less excitedly we can get down
before God, the more easily are we truly guidable. "The meek will
He guide in judgment; and the meek will He teach His way"
(Ps. 25: 9).

Take, now, the second of our three "cautions", i.e. the danger
of following mere *"impressions"*. Many Christians, besides having
the new spiritual life which comes by regeneration, have an old
sentimental streak in their nature by heredity, from which, like
moonlight vapours from a tropical swamp, emotional responses
rise up through the spiritual, and seem like "guidance from
above", when they are merely impressions from within! Even
persons of an *un*sentimental cast, too, in seasons of spiritual intensity or when seeking guidance during emotional stress, may
similarly fall prey to mistaking mere impressions for divine

guidance. Indeed, what could seem *likelier* than that those inward "voices" which come during sacred seasons of communion are from heaven? Well, some of them are; but not necessarily all. The way to make sure is to ask: Does this "voice" or "impression" harmonize?—that is, does it harmonize with God's *other* voices? God's voices to the human spirit, in Scripture, conscience, circumstance, and inward urge, are never divergent notes, but always a blending chord. However clanging an inner "impression" may be, if it grates against those other voices, or offends our sense of moral right, it is not of God. Let us never *insist* that an inner urge is of the Holy Spirit if it strikes a discord, or savours of "self" in any way, for Ezekiel 13: 3 says, "Woe unto the foolish prophets that follow their own spirit and have seen nothing!"

And now, our third "caution": the commonest *mistake* which people make, in soliciting divine guidance, is to think that guidance comes only by *abnormal* means. It must be a flash from the sky, a voice out of space, a vision in the night, a strange freak of circumstance, a supernatural omen, or else (supposedly) it cannot be divine guidance! Some of the Lord's dear children would do well to learn, once and for all, these two facts: (1) in this present age, with its complete Bible, and the Holy Spirit Himself indwelling each born-again believer, God uses abnormal means of guidance less than ever; (2) the less you and I *need* abnormal signs and tokens, the better able are we to be guided *continually* by the indwelling Holy Spirit, as He applies the written Word, and interprets circumstances to our illumined reason.

Some time ago, a friend of mine was showing me round his estate. We walked by a small field in which some handsome Arabian horses were feeding, and I could not resist tempting them to come to me at the wire fence. My friend said, "They want to come, but they won't. You'll soon know why if you put your hand on the wire fence". That wire fence was mildly electrified. Just one contact of their noses with that fence, and those horses knew to keep away! It may seem a far cry from those horses to this matter of divine guidance; yet as I stood there that day, and touched that wire fence, and my hand twinged at the sensation of the electric current, I found myself thinking that, after all, the highést and truest form of guidance is not that which comes by intermittent abnormalities, but that which comes *continually* by the electric current of the Holy Spirit flowing through our own consecrated faculties of reason and conscience. When our mental and moral faculties are really consecrated to Christ, *then* the Holy Spirit can guide us best of all through our own natural faculties. Moreover, this is a guidance which goes on, all the while, amid the incidentals of "the daily round and common task" as well as at those critical junctures when life's bigger decisions have to be made.

Whenever I think of those persons who are always wanting abnormal "signs" or supernatural interposings before they can believe that guidance has come, I am reminded of a sentence which I read in a magazine, years ago: "Everyone needs two conversions; one from the natural into the supernatural, and another from the supernatural back into the natural!" The more *naturally* we allow ourselves to be guided by the Holy Spirit, the better. I fully realise that divine guidance, just because it *is* divine, is *super*natural; yet the fact remains that in the case of the Christian believer, indwelt by the Holy Spirit, the intendedly normal way of guidance is for the Holy Spirit to guide the consecrated believer through the natural functioning of enlightened perception, reason, judgment, conscience, decision.

For instance, when some opportunity of doing good confronts us, the normal movement of the Holy Spirit is to incline us toward it through our natural responses. No abnormal guidance is needed. It is perfectly in line with the written Word: "To him that knoweth to do good, and doeth it not, to him it is sin" (Jas. 4: 17). In such cases, declining to act until the Spirit "moves" us is not spiritual-mindedness, but "self" in a pious-looking mask. Similarly, when golden opportunities of witnessing for Christ present themselves, the normal movement of the Holy Spirit is to incline us toward discreetly making the most of them. No abnormal guidance is needed. Yet I have met some brethren, quite recently, who said it was presumption ever to speak in such circumstances without being specially "moved" by the Spirit. (The result of this, as enquiry showed me, was that they were *never* "moved" by the Spirit.) To be always requiring guidance by abnormal signs, urges, and "movings of the Spirit" is not a mark of deeper spirituality, but of spiritual immaturity.

Those Three Guiding Lights

Little recapitulation is needed on how to *recognise* divine guidance. We do well to recall again and again the F. B. Meyer story about those three big lights on the Liverpool shore. When (1) the written Word, and (2) the inward urge, and (3) the corroboration of outward circumstances, all blend in one, then we need have no fear; guidance is clear. It is not necessary that all three should always positively coincide; but there should never be any real contradiction between them; and if there should be even a *seeming* contradiction between them, we should wait for more light, rather than presume. And always, in the last analysis, inward "pressure" and outward "pointer" must be tested by written Scripture.

There is an Old Testament incident which rather strikingly illustrates this complementary blending of all three. It occurs in First Samuel, and tells how Saul was guided to become the first king of Israel. First, there was *the Word of God* through Samuel: "The Lord hath anointed thee to be captain over His inheritance" (10: 1). Second, there came an *inward moving* from the Holy Spirit: "The Spirit of God came upon him, and he prophesied" (10). Third, there was *outward corroboration*: "And all those signs [see 3–5] came to pass that day" (9).

Reverting again, for a moment, to our remark that inward "pressure" and outward "pointer" must needs be tested by the written Scripture, we ought to add this modifying word: it is *not* necessary always to have (as some affirm) an actual *verse* or some actual *wording* of the Bible to confirm every important decision. The Bible itself nowhere lays down such a requirement. Nor does it denote special reverence in ourselves that we should demand such verbal endorsement. Would we dare to say that God has never spoken directly to men since the canon of Scripture was closed? Would we dare to say that God never speaks today except in the literal syllables of Holy Writ? Surely not! We are to test inward urge and outward sign by the *sense* of Scripture.

Some Final Considerations

Finally, here are a few further aspects which should at least be mentioned. Let us remember that when we are sincerely fulfilling the simple conditions, we must have *faith* that guidance will come (1 John 5: 14, 15). "Without faith we cannot please God" (Heb. 11: 6). We may do more than merely hope. We should expect.

Again, we should exercise *patience,* believing, when there seems delay, that the Holy Spirit never wastes our time. We should believe and wait calmly. Excitement or impatience betokens defective yieldedness. The waiting of one extra day may show how near we were to some serious mistake.

Again, when guidance comes, we should believe it, and not tantalize ourselves by asking if, after all, this *is* the guidance. If it fits the tests, we need not be paralysed by indecision.

By way of parting reminder, also, let us ever remember that *continual* guidance is dependent on spiritual *maturity*. See again Romans 8: 14, "As many as are led by the Spirit of God, they are the *sons* of God", i.e. grown sons, as distinct from immature minors. We need to be continually yielded to Christ, and habitually prayerful. Guidance and prayerlessness never go together. With ample reason W. E. Sangster says: "It could turn one alternately to laughter or tears, to find people fully admitting the need to set several hours aside daily to master shorthand or a foreign language, and blandly supposing that they can conquer sin and know God by a few sleepy moments at the end of the day."

Furthermore, although there *is* a place for "extraordinary" guidance, do not seek it. If God deems it needful it will come. Leave that to Him. Seek, rather, to be so yielded to our dear Lord, so spiritually mature, and so susceptible to the Holy Spirit, that there can be direct communication, Spirit to spirit, all the time. It certainly was "extraordinary" guidance when our Lord Jesus was "driven" by the Holy Spirit to be tempted of Satan in the wilderness; and so it was when Philip was guided away from the revival movement in Samaria to the lonely road between Jerusalem and Gaza—to intercept the Ethiopian chancellor (Acts 8); but such interpositions of "extraordinary" guidance usually have to do with special divine *purpose*, rather than special human *asking*.

Will it sound a little unusual if we also add: do not think that divine guidance always means doing something *hard*. I have known Christian friends who, if they were not quite sure which way guidance pointed, would obligingly give the Lord "the benefit of the doubt", assuming that whichever of the two choices was the hard way must be the Lord's way! Nay; divine guidance is meant to *guard* us, not *scourge* us!

Also, if we are truly walking in fellowship with our dear Master, let us give over suspecting the sincerity of our own *desires*! How many true saints there are who are sure that divine guidance must necessarily run opposite to their own desires, no matter how sincere those desires may be! Read Psalm 37: 4, again. To the sanctified, guidance *often* comes through their own desires; for those very desires are begotten within them by the Holy Spirit as one of His lovelier ways of impressing and directing.

In connection with all this we cannot emphasize too strongly the spiritual *maturity,* already mentioned, which makes us continually *susceptible* to the direct leading of the Holy Spirit. Such maturity, with its accompanying sensitivity to the communicated mind of the heavenly Spirit, never develops in any but the habitually prayerful. If we would live guidedly we *must* make time for *God.* Not all the theories or mechanics of guidance ever propounded can take the place of that. One of the uncooperative ironies of our present life is, that *bad* habits grow of their own accord and have to be resisted, whereas good habits must be deliberately formed and nurtured, often with patient perseverance and resolute self-discipline. That is true of habitual prayer. It requires (especially at first) godly resolve and perseverance (though how rich the rewards later!). Let me sympathetically urge that if it is at all possible, the *best* time for the day's first "set season" of prayer is early morning, when our faculties are freshest, and before the day's absorptions or distractions have come crowding in. The whole day is wonderfully affected by that anticipative early "morning watch" at the gates of the heavenly Wisdom; and, more than anything else, it engenders true susceptibility to divine guidance.

We shall have more to say later about prayer in relation to guidance, but while we are here touching on this strategy of the *early morning* prayer-time let me give one further quotation from W. E. Sangster's virile little book on the subject.[1]

"Some people complain that they are not really *awake* in the early morning, even if they get up. A sponge under the cold tap will help. Get up! No charge of vagueness can be brought against this advice. Get up! 'Make conscience of *beginning* the day with God,' said Bunyan. And one of the best ways of beginning the day well is to begin it the night before. Earlier rising may require earlier retiring. Wesley is said to have left the company of Dr. Johnson because it was near his bed-time. He had an appointment with God at 4 a.m. and he would not risk the perils of over-sleeping for the greatest littérateur of the age. . . . Francis Asbury rose

---

[1] *God Does Guide Us.*

at five o'clock and spent his first hour in prayer. . . . Andrew
Bonar said, 'Unless I get up to the measure of at least two hours
in *pure prayer* every day I shall not be satisfied.' In the light of
all this, is it too much to ask for *one* hour a day for our devotions?
. . . To make free use of the word 'guidance', with no such background of daily devotion, is to misapply a precious and awesome
term, and to bring it into disrepute. God does not treat us as
dictaphones. His guidance is given on conditions. He has guided
seekers and saints in every age, but, with all the variations of
circumstances, their quest and conquest had this in common—
they gave God time."

Some time ago, when I was gratefully thinking over this matter
of guidance, I found my thoughts shaping themselves into a short
hymn, which now, perhaps, may make a fitting prayer as we
close these reflections, together.

> Lord, help me clearly understand,
> My way is all by Thee foreplanned ;
> And I, full-yielding to Thy will,
> Life's richest purpose may fulfil.
>
> With each new winding of the way,
> New guidance may be mine each day ;
> A yielded heart in daily prayer
> Discerns Thy watch-care everywhere.
>
> Each day, as I with Thee commune,
> Lord, set my heart and mind attune,
> To hear the inward Voice divine,
> With scarce a need for outward sign.
>
> So, guided through my earthly days,
> Safeguarded thus from error's maze,
> My heav'nward pilgrimage shall be
> A deepening fellowship with Thee.

SO, WHAT ABOUT IT?

Religion, when it is fresh and vital, is never afraid either of the cost or of the possible risk of direct inspiration; but when it cools it wants rules and systems, wants to avoid the personal searching which is needed to find direct inspiration, wants to avoid the clash with the conventional world and the conventional church, and the hazard to one's own personal security which is incidental upon living in the Spirit. Jesus did not let men rest content with memories. He made them look forward to a time when His human voice would be withdrawn, and the command of His lips could be no longer heard; when His Church was to be dependent upon the Holy Spirit, who should call to our minds the things He said, take of the things of Christ and show them to the world in fresh ways which the world could understand. The Holy Spirit's guidance will never be contrary to the New Testament: it will really show us what the New Testament means for us in any given case.

Samuel M. Shoemaker.

6

SO, WHAT ABOUT IT?

FORTY years ago this year, I became wedded to the dearest, sweetest girl in our town. After the service in the church, we went into the minister's vestry, accompanied by our parents, to sign the marriage register. After the signing, my dear mother gave me a kiss, adding, with a whimsical look, "Well, Sid, my only son, you are now married. You are at the end of all your troubles—*this* end"! Then she gave us a text from the Bible, which she hoped would be a life-long motto. It was Proverbs 3: 5, 6, especially the words, "In all thy ways acknowledge *HIM*, and He shall direct thy paths."

Ever since then those two verses have had a peculiarly affecting meaning for me. I never read them or reflect on them but (as the old song says) "her voice comes floating o'er the air", and I hear again the kindly tones of "a voice now still", softly repeating the words to us. I like the text best as the Septuagint Version brought it over from the Hebrew to the Greek in the third century B.C.

> "Trust in the Lord with all thine heart,
>   And lean not to thine own understanding;
>   In all thy ways acknowledge Him,
>   And He shall *RIGHTLY DIVIDE* thy paths."

"Rightly Divide"!

The apostle uses the same Greek word in 2 Timothy 2: 15, where he says, "Study to show thyself approved unto God, a workman that needeth not to be ashamed, *RIGHTLY DIVIDING* the Word of truth." The greek verb is *orthotomeo*, a compound of *orthos* (right) and *temno* (to cut), meaning to cut apart rightly.

Could *any* mother ever give a more suitable wedding text to a young couple than Proverbs 3: 5, 6? It consists of three sage counsels, crowned by one excelsior promise—a promise which makes the three counsels richly prophetic to all who heed them. The three counsels are: (1) "Trust Jehovah with all thy heart,"

(2) "Rely not on thine own insight," (3) "In all thy ways acknowledge Him." The crowning promise is:

"AND HE SHALL RIGHTLY DIVIDE THY PATHS"

As for that third counsel ("In all thy ways acknowledge Him") the word "all" is certainly notable. It covers the whole area of human activity—mental, moral, spiritual, physical, sacred, secular, domestic, commercial, public and private. It means that we are to acknowledge God not only in formal acts of religious worship, or when outstanding emergencies drive us urgently to Him for help, but in all our dealings and activities, down to those which in *our* estimation may seem almost trivial.

Most of us Christian believers realize our need of divine guidance in the big things, such as marriage, choice of career, a business partnership, change of occupation, a new house to live in, the planning of long or important travel, the engaging in some special form of Christian service, the removal to a new town or country, the Yes or No to some surgical operation; but (although perhaps we would not say so in spoken word) we secretly think it incredulous that guidance by the infinite God reaches down to the details of our "daily round and common task". That lurking incredulity is wrong if Proverbs 3: 5, 6, is right.

As soon as we start *loving* another human person, we start *caring* for that person. Loving always expresses itself in caring. That is just as true of God as it is of ourselves, though in a measurelessly sublimer way. If the Bible is true, and if the teaching of our Lord Jesus, the incarnate divine Son, is true, then God loves *each* of us with an individualizing concentration; not just *all* of us in a kind of general way. The wonder which thrilled Paul was: "The Son of God loved *me*, and gave Himself for *me*" (Gal. 2: 20). Well, the same price which was paid for Paul's redemption was paid for yours and mine. You, *as* you, and I, as I, are uniquely dear to God; and because He loves us individually He *cares* for us individually, with a care reaching into everything which concerns us. Both by creation and redemption we are meant for *fellowship* with God; and guidance—continually asked for and continually given—is one of the richest interplays of fellowship between God and human hearts.

So, as Moses stood and wondered before the burning bush on Horeb, you and I may well stand and gratefully wonder again at this resplendent divine pledge of guidance: "He shall *RIGHTLY*

DIVIDE thy paths." How often, as we encounter day-by-day experiences, we need guidance, not merely between the right and the wrong, between the wise and the unwise, but between several choices all of which are morally right, all seemingly reasonable, yet among which only one is in the direct line of the divine purpose to bless; only one which will fulfil some vital ministry of the Holy Spirit through us! How those ways need to be "rightly divided" for us!

"He shall *rightly divide* thy paths." With this promise shining in upon our minds afresh, let us here finally review the more salient features pertaining to divine guidance. Some of these we have touched on already. Any brief re-mention here is simply as part of our summary reflection on the whole subject.

The Reality of It

To begin with, let our findings thus far abolish doubt once for all as to the *reality* of divine guidance. Though the stars in God's universe outnumber all the grains of sand on all the earth's sea-shores, the God who made those galaxies galore has revealed Himself in Christ as your heavenly *Father*. Listen no longer to the materialistic philosopher who laughs at man's littleness against the staggering colossus of the physical creation. Even here on earth, one precious *child* bearing the family likeness means far more to any noble father than the mansion he has built for himself; more than all his lands and estates and other material possessions. You are God's *child*. He calls you so. He loves you as such. His will is ever for your wellbeing. In that will He wants to *guide* you. Jesus knew the vastness of God better than any modern scientist, for He "came forth from God" (John 16: 28), yet it is He who, more than anyone else, sees the presence of God everywhere, with His fatherhood entering into every human detail. Learn to sing with F. W. Faber,

> My God, how wonderful Thou art!
> Thy majesty how bright!
> How beautiful Thy mercy seat
> In depths of burning light!
>
> How dread are Thine eternal years,
> O everlasting Lord,
> By prostrate spirits, day and night,
> Incessantly adored!

> Yet I may love Thee too, O Lord,
>   Almighty as Thou art;
> For Thou hast stooped to *ask* of me
>   The love of my poor heart!

> No earthly father loves like Thee,
>   No mother half so mild
> Bears and forbears as Thou hast done
>   With me, Thy sinful *child*.

"This God is *our* God for ever and ever: He will be our *Guide* even unto death" (Ps. 48: 14). "The Father Himself loveth you" (John 16: 27). "He will guide you" (16: 13).

The Guidance Level

There is such a thing as living on the guidance *level*. Indeed, it is necessary to live on that level if guidance is to be a continuous experience. It has been truly said that there are three levels on which men live: (1) the level of natural desire, impulse, or instinct—the "I *want* level; (2) the higher level of conscience, of moral scruple, or sense of duty—the "I *ought* level; (3) the highest level, that of regeneration, of the new life in Christ, of yieldedness to God—the "I am *led*" level.

Even at best, on the two lower levels any guidance is misty or foggy. If it is given at all it has to be the kind given to mules— forced, rather than intelligently understood. To those who think that acting according to conscience is more or less equal to divine guidance we only need mention zealous but unconverted Saul of Tarsus who was devoutly following his religious conscience in persecuting the Church and slaying the early Christians. Saul's conscience and God's will were in sheer opposition, not because Saul's conscience had suddenly gone rotten, but simply because it was *misguided*.

It should be the master-passion of every Christian to live on that sunlit upper level where intelligence, instinct, conscience, free-will, intention and activity are all kept in the line of God's directive purpose; where heavenly fellowship and guidance are therefore continuous. Most of us need to rise above mere *interval* guidance—emergency requests for it at points of acute need or crisis, with intervening gaps of self-management. Our sacred ambition should be a minute-by-minute *life* guidance, on that top level of entire sanctification.

The Joy of It

That brings us to mention the *joy* of living in such realized guidance. Fellowship with God means nothing to the worldling, but it is "heaven begun below" to the Christian. Guidance from God is inconceivable to the materialist, but it is "joy unspeakable" to the spiritually minded. The Christian life begins with "the joy of sins forgiven, of peace with God, of guilt washed away, and pledge of heaven," but it reaches its purest ecstasy in *"fellowship* with the Father and with His Son" (1 John 1: 3). Such fellowship *includes* that spirit-to-spirit guidance which fills the consecrated heart with a song unknown to others. Think of Fanny Crosby, singing with inward radiance amid life-long physical blindness,

> All the way my Saviour *leads* me,
>   What have I to ask beside?
> Can I doubt His tender mercy
>   Who through life has been my *Guide*?
> Heavenly peace, divinest comfort,
>   Here by faith in Him to dwell;
> For I know, whate'er befall me,
>   Jesus doeth all things well.

Some of those dear old hymns about divine guidance have acquired a deeper meaning for me during the past twelve years of almost non-stop travel all over the North American Continent and in other parts of the world. There has had to be a planning ahead, a prayerful selecting of bookings, a trusting for needs to be met, a timing and mapping of travel, and an anticipative guidance not required in the settled pastorate. Again and again my dear wife and I have had to "sing for joy of heart" (Isa. 65: 14) at the evidence of heavenly planning. I wonder whether there can be any higher joy on earth than a continually living in conscious God-guidedness.

The Cost of It

Yet we must guard against a one-sided impression. Besides thè joy of guidance there is the *cost* of it. Mrs. Hannah Whitall Smith is well worth quoting here: "Remember that God has all knowledge and all wisdom, and that therefore it is very possible He may guide you into paths wherein *He* knows great blessings are awaiting you, but which, to the short-sighted human eyes around you, seem sure to result in confusion and loss. You must recognize the fact that God's thoughts are not as man's thoughts, nor His ways as man's ways; and that He alone, who knows the end of things from the beginning, can judge what the results of any course of action may be. You must therefore realize that His very love for you may perhaps lead you to run counter to the loving wishes of even your dearest friends. You must learn, from Luke 14: 26–33 and similar passages, that in order to be a disciple and follower of your Lord you may perhaps be called upon to forsake inwardly all that you have, even father or mother, or brother or sister, or husband or wife, or it may be your own life also. Unless the possibility of this is clearly recognized, you will be very likely to get into difficulty."

That is wisely spoken. Unpreparedness for the disapproval of those whom we love or esteem can trip us into sudden quandary, or sting us with toxic doubts about the Lord's leading. Face it: there may be a price to pay for going all the way with the revealed will of God; but be assured that those who go right through with Him have a song of joy all the more soaring because of tests surmounted. Such going through with divine guidance wonderfully develops spiritual *maturity*, and who would not rather live in the intelligence of adulthood than remain locked in the ignorance of a static childhood.

The Voice From Heaven

We should cultivate, also, an aptness to distinguish the voice of the Holy Spirit. To a prayerful heart, with an open Bible at hand, this is not difficult; but it is always important, and can be a sensitive problem to the inexperienced. There are other "voices", impressions, suggestions, which may *seem* to be His, unless we are practised in discernment. The opinions, advice, influence, of those around us, especially those of dominant persuasiveness or those whose judgment we value, can set up inward reactions which *seem* to be from the Holy Spirit. Also, when imagination is active, subtle autosuggestion can imitate the divine urge. Furthermore, much as we may dislike referring to it, there are evil spirits, confederates of Satan (Eph. 2: 2) who, although they cannot see inside our human minds (only God can do that) may inject disguised false constraints through our natural susceptibilities.

How, then, may we surely recognize the true voice of the Holy Spirit? First, if any supposed "guidance" contradicts prayerful *intelligence*, it is wrong. True guidance, other than excluding the exercise of our own keen, practical judgment, invites it. Often it concurs with it. Sometimes it transcends it. But it never violently collides with it. No course of action which insults plain common-sense can be of the Holy Spirit.

Nor is true guidance ever *erratic*. Any urge to act precipitately, hurriedly, drastically must be ejected from our minds as an ill-working foreigner. We may be truly guided to act promptly, but never hastily, much less rashly. Quietness, calmness, a deep, unhurried assurance; those are the hall-marks of genuine guidance.

Give the Book Priority

Above all else, the Bible must be our criterion. So far as all other voices are concerned, we may say, as in Isaiah 8: 20, "If they speak not according to this Word, it is because there is no light in them." If we act on "inner voices" without testing them by the teaching of Holy Scripture we soon become a prey to delusion or run into chaotic error. *How* do we test urges and impressions by Scripture? Since the Bible does not mention by name or give a specific rule for every matter which arises, how do we test the guidance which has to come to us from *outside* of it? Let me quote Mrs. Hannah W. Smith again:

"The Scriptures are far more explicit, even about details, than most people think; and there are not many important affairs in life for which a clear direction may not be found in God's book. Take the matter of dress, and we have 1 Peter 3: 3, 4, with 1 Timothy 2: 9. Take the matter of conversation, and we have Ephesians 4: 29, and 5: 4. Take the matter of avenging injuries or standing up for our rights, and we have Romans 12: 19–21, Matthew 5: 38–48, and 1 Peter 2: 19–21. Take the matter of forgiving one another, and we have Ephesians 4: 32 with Mark 11: 25, 26. Take the matter of conformity to the 'world', and we have Romans 12: 2, with 1 John 2: 15–17, and James 4: 4. Take the matter of anxieties of every kind, and we have Matthew 6: 25–34, and Philippians 4: 6, 7."

These Biblical *specifics* might be considerably extended. It is surprising how many matters of present-day concern the Bible *does* prescribe for. So, of course, in seeking guidance, we ought always to ascertain whether there is any direct Biblical reference to whatever it is which perplexes us. If there is not, then it will certainly be covered by some Biblical *principle*. The Bible is "a book of principles" not of "disjointed aphorisms"; and the *principles* taught in Scripture cover every detail which can ever present itself in our quest for divine direction.

For instance, modern trade unions are not mentioned in the Bible, nor are television, present-day politics, or certain recent social innovations; but the Christian attitude towards them, or behaviour amid them, is very clearly indicated by the general *tenor,* or cumulative *force,* or directional *drive,* or moral *standards* of Holy Writ. Above all else, in this matter of guided living, the Bible gives us divine *principles of action,* and these are often better than having a thing mentioned by name, because they give us the *moral reason* for our attitude or course of action.

The *principles* of Scripture are often better tests of guidance than isolated texts. Perhaps not all of us need the following counsel, but some of us do, namely: in appropriating some particular text as guidance, we should be careful not to play it off against other Scriptures, or read into it a meaning which it does not really have. I have read of a Christian woman who was so convinced of guidance from the words, "All things are yours" (1 Cor. 3: 21) that she went with happy assurance and stole somebody else's money in order to refund a friend to whom it was owing! She would have been spared the grievous results of this if she had only read her guidance-text against the background of Scripture principles in general! Such gullibility as that dear sister's often contradicts Scripture under the very guise of obeying it!

All of this leads me to add that those are best prepared for true guidance who know the Bible most fully and familiarly. I am not denying that the Holy Spirit *does* at times guide us by an actual text of Scripture; but we must never use the wording of any particular text in a way which conflicts with Scripture teaching as a whole.

The Discipline of Waiting

Be prepared for the healthy discipline of *waiting.* Never think that guidance delayed is guidance denied. Many have left on record their testimony that those times when they were kept waiting for clear guidance have sometimes proved, in the end, more educative than the guidance itself. Looking back over my own fairly diversified experience, I can gratefully vouch that again and again, when guidance for some problematical situation has seemed disappointingly slow in coming, and I have been tempted to allow feelings of irreverent impatience, the situation itself has unexpectedly changed during the seeming hold-up, making my first-requested guidance no longer relevant. At the same time I have seen how unhappy the result would have been if I had not waited, but had acted in my ignorance of how events were going to turn.

I am also bound to testify that some of those wait . . . wait . . . and still wait periods have been among the most sanctifying and enriching episodes of my pilgrimage. The heart-searching and examining of motives which they have provoked; the prayerfulness and deepened sense of dependence on God which they have induced; the inward stillness and assurance and clearer fellowship with God which they have begotten; these have been rewards which have exceeded in preciousness even the guidance itself for which I was lingering! One day, away back in my youth, I was in a hen-run belonging to a friend of mine. Suspended in a string-bag from the branch of a tree was some edible substance which was evidently very tasty to the hens, for they kept jumping up and pecking at it, one after another. When I asked my friend why he kept it tantalizingly hanging above them instead of on the ground, he laughed. "It's put there for a purpose," he said. "These little hens of mine need *exercise*, and that's one way of making sure that they get it." I have never forgotten it. How often we wonder why something dearly wanted or keenly needed seems kept just beyond our reach! Little do we realize God's good purpose in this. What spiritual exercise it causes! How it develops us in our Christian life! It often means that as well as guiding us, God is *training* us.

Avoid Dictating "Signs"

Not many of us, I would hope, need this further word of counsel; but for the sake of the few who may, here it is. If guidance seems withheld or obscure for a time, we should never try to force an answer from God by requiring Him to give a sign in some way which we ourselves devise. "Dear Lord, I am going to take it as Thy guidance if that person 'phones me before eleven o'clock tomorrow morning." Or, "Lord, if such-and-such a thing doesn't happen to stop me on Friday, I will take it as Thy sign that I am to go right on with this thing."

Such sign-dictating is both presumptuous and hazardous.

Gideon and his fleece are no safe example to us. Signs and miracles of that kind are seldom if ever needed today. We have a completed Bible such as Gideon never knew. We live in the full light of Christian revelation, which Gideon did not. At the time of the fleece incident Gideon had only just been converted from the Baal-worship apostasy, and he had no earlier experience of the true God to fall back on. The faith which always needs supernatural "signs and wonders" is still in the kindergarten.

I am not saying that there is no place at all for signs; but I *am* saying that since Scripture revelation became completed, and the Spirit of God Himself came to indwell all Christian believers, there is not the same need for that long-ago *kind* of sign. Also, I *am* saying that to invent signs of our own and then, so to speak, corner God into using *them* for our guidance, is a manipulating of things which is as risky as it is unauthorized.

Group Guidance

At this point it may be useful to insert a word about *group* guidance. Although on an earlier page we have advised against being overly swayed by the natural urge of those around us, it is our wisdom to recognize that in many a situation there is a true place for such "group" guidance. Of course, everything depends on the spiritual qualification of the group. Divine guidance comes through a group only when the group itself is divinely guided. It is not just the human advice even of spiritually minded Christian believers which constitutes group guidance. Those who compose the group or circle must themselves be earnestly waiting on God, so that real guidance about the matter in question may come to us through their united impression or conviction. Anything short of that can scarcely be called group *"guidance"*.

Provided we are clear as to that, it may be wise, in certain circumstances, to check our own individual inference of guidance with discreet, praying confidants. Solitary, individualistic interpretation of guidance can, and sometimes does, "run off the rails" or stray into unwise courses. Prayerful Christian companions can often be God's true intermediaries of guidance to us. Sometimes they can interpret the factors in a "situation" of ours better than we ourselves can, because they are outside the emotional centre of it, and can see things more objectively. I am reminded of a certain gifted minister who, out of a sense of loyalty, stayed on in a certain place where, because of neighbourhood and other changes, his ministry was cramped, almost crippled, and his needed influence in a wider area was sacrificed. Some of us who often prayed for him were one in a sincere conviction that he should seek a change. When he said, "I simply will not leave here until I get clear guidance from God," we were brave enough to reply, "Has it never occurred to you that God may be guiding you through brethren who love you and pray for you?" Later he came to see that God had indeed been giving him "group" guidance.

Yes, group guidance; yet we must sound a tocsin. Beware lest confiding in this and that and the other friend becomes a subtle distribution of information which borders on confidential gossip; and be sure that those in whom you confide are consecrated intercessors, not whisperers to others. I remember a woman who was deeply troubled about the godless behaviour of her husband. Things reached a point where she certainly needed more than human guidance as to how she should relate herself to his behaviour. The supreme need was to win him for Christ, but when, through a slip of someone's tongue, he learned that his wife had been distributing intimate information about him of which he was ashamed, it so discouraged him that he turned completely away. Her confiding in friends had been ostensibly for the purpose of getting their intercessions and prayerful advice, but it had become an advertising of personal misdoings which rarely if ever should be confided to others.

So, if "group" guidance has to swing into play—and it has a real ministry—any kind of personal exposures must be kept to a sheer minimum, not only for the sake of the person concerned, but for our Lord's sake. Any such communications simply *must* be kept strictly to the very fewest among really trustable Christian confidants—experienced believers who are known for their discretion and prayerfulness.

Guidance Through Sanctified Desires

Above all else, we should earnestly covet that guidance from Heaven which comes through our own *sanctified desires*. I used to think that the highest point in the Christian life is that at which we are willing to forgo our own will in favour of God's, whatever the cost. But there is a higher point even than that. In fact, it is the highest point of all. It is our loving God so dearly that we never even *desire* that which is not His will. When we love God like that there is no need for self-wrestling to give up something which *we* want but which is not in accord with *God's* will. If we *did* want any such thing, the very learning that it was not according to His will would at once take away all our desire for it. Yes, that is the highest point—where we so love and desire what our glorious Lord loves and desires that there is never *any* clash of will.

It is the point, the place, the level, of utter yieldedness to Him, of deep-going inward renewal of our whole mental and moral nature by the Holy Spirit; of "living" and "walking" in the Spirit. It is that experience of unclouded fellowship with God in which we know in fullest degree the guidance indicated in Philippians 2: 13 and Hebrews 13: 21—"It is God who worketh *in you* both to *will* and to *do* of His good pleasure"; "The God of peace . . . perfect you in every good work to do *His* will. Himself working *in you* that which is well-pleasing in His sight."

Oh, that is the maturest and holiest form of divine guidance! It is guidance on the highest of all levels, and it makes life wonderful. It is guidance, not so much deciphered from external signs or pointers, nor inferred from unusual internal pressures, but guidance gently, unobstructedly revealing itself through inwrought holy *desires*. It is this which makes the will of God "the perfect law of *liberty*" to us (Jas. 1: 25). Our continual *choosing* of God's will is as easy as the *doing* of it is sometimes made hard by unsympathetic circumstances. In our hearts there is rich and satisfying answer to the prayer—

> Breathe on me, Breath of God,
>   Fill me with life anew,
> That I may *love* what *Thou* dost love
>   And *do* what *Thou* wouldst do.

Psalm 37 becomes a living reality in our experience: "Delight thyself in the Lord and He shall give thee the *desires* of thine heart. Commit thy way unto the Lord; trust also in Him, and He shall bring it to pass." God's will and our walk coincide. Thus He now guides by *drawing* us, without need for *driving* us. We find Romans 8: 14 coming alive to us: "As many as are *led* by the Spirit of God, they are the sons of God." There is no more elevated experience on this earth than to go through one's days and hours with an unbroken sense of such God-guidedness. With

such experience of guidance on our pilgrimage to the celestial city
we break into songs like F. W. Faber's—

> I have no cares, O blessed Will,
>   For all my cares are Thine;
> I live in triumph, Lord, for Thou
>   Hast made Thy triumph mine.

> Ill, by Thy blessing, is my good,
>   And unblest good is ill;
> And all is right that seems most wrong,
>   If it be Thy sweet will.

SOME FINALLY EMERGENT REMINDERS

And now, as we conclude this first half of our chapters on
guidance, perhaps we may usefully bind a few finalizing paragraphs into a sheaf of pensive reminders.

We Christian believers should develop the habit of viewing all
our earthly concerns as we shall view them when the time comes
for us to leave this present life and pass into the Beyond. When
at length we "cross the river" and ascend yonder shining approach
to the heavenly city, will some of us give wistful looks backward,
wishing we had lived our days on earth differently? Many of the
pursuits and anxieties which largely absorb our time *now* may
look pitifully small *then*; but there will be no coming back to
correct our folly. How loyal we ought to be, despite all discouragements, in daily witnessing for the Saviour! How deeply concerned
we should be about putting Him first in all our choices! How
earnestly should we determine on living a God-guided life! To
have acknowledged Jesus as King, yet to have preferred the
dictates of our own erring self-wisdom, will seem strangely contradictory and blameworthy as we go to *meet* Him.

Further, as any enlightened Christian mind can see, to live in
the guiding will of God, besides being a mark of spirituality, is
obvious *common sense*. Think again: God knows us better than
our nearest relatives or dearest friends; better than we know ourselves; every breath, every heart-beat, every thought, word, act,
all our life through. He knew us anticipatively before the world
was; and He will know us omnisciently throughout the entire
futurity of our being. As the awed psalmist says in contemplating
this, "Thou understandest my thought afar off"—i.e. even in its

embryonic evolvings. In a word, God knows us absolutely. What blind misuse of human independence it is for any of us knowingly to live in disregard of *that*!

Equally plainly, living in the accepted guidance of God is the way of *peace*. David knew this when he sang, "He *leadeth* me beside the *still* waters". Admittedly, there is no guarantee that living inside divine guidance invariably ensures placidity of *outward* circumstances; but it always brings *inward* repose. Frequently, in strange-seeming providences, God's truly guided mariners are allowed to run into stormy waters. Sometimes the most signally guided path of devoutest pilgrims may wind through sinister ambushes of evil or areas of outward provocation. This is exemplified repeatedly in prominent Bible characters, most notably perhaps in the travel episodes of Paul. But the well-documented paradox is, that when the outer agitation grows roughest, the peace within is deepest (see Acts 23: 11 with 2 Tim. 4: 16–18 and Phil. 4: 6, 7).

In one of its lovelier spiritual aspects, the God-guided life is that of the *manifested Presence*. Are there few or many among believers today who experience frequent fulfilments of our Lord's promise in John 14: 21?—"He that loveth Me shall be loved of my Father . . . and I will *manifest* Myself to Him". Oh, with what joy it gilds our days when with inward luminousness we realize His presence within us! What comfort was that revealed presence to Paul as he stood his trial before Nero! "At my first defence no man stood with me, but all forsook me. . . . Notwithstanding, the Lord stood with me, and strengthened me."

Think of "Brother Lawrence", the seventeenth-century kitchen servant. "The time of business does not with me differ from the time of prayer; and in the noise and clutter of my kitchen, while several persons are at the same time calling for different things, I possess God in as great tranquillity as if I were on my knees. . . . I make it my business only to persevere in His holy presence, wherein I keep myself by a simple attention and an habitual, silent and secret conversation of the soul with God, which often causes me joys and raptures inwardly, and sometimes outwardly, so great that I am forced to use means to moderate them and prevent their appearance to others . . . There is not in the world a kind of life more sweet and delightful than that of a continual conversation with God. Those only can comprehend it who practise and experience it."

Finally, we may add that only a God-guided life fulfils the intention of divine *election*. In the New Testament epistles we are told that the redeemed who compose the true Church, our Lord's mystic body, were "chosen in Him before the foundation of the world", and that those whom God "did foreknow" He also "did predestinate". Is it not plainly revealed in those same inspired oracles that the eternity *before* time and the eternity *after* time are both linked by a divine purpose running right *through* time? (Rom. 8: 28, Eph. 1: 9, 2 Tim. 1: 9, Titus 1: 2, etc.) Does that purpose accidentally *overlook* any of us?

We know, of course, that our race has fallen from the higher level of God's *directive* will to the lower level of His *permissive* will, and that in this intermediate succession of time-ages there is an accommodated *overruling* of permitted evils which God never *directly* purposed (for God cannot be the author of evil). Nevertheless the Davids and Jeremiahs and (as already noted) even that poor, blind beggar of John 9: 3 are written in God's pre-cosmic "book", to fulfil predesigned intention. There is mystery about it all; yet enough is revealed to make these deductions firm.

In greater or lesser degree we may *thwart* the divine purpose for our earthly years. Human free-will is a fact. Sin is a fact. God's *permissive* will is as much a fact in the lives of human individuals as it is in the sweep of the centuries. Never for a moment must we think that everything which happens to human individuals is predetermined by God. There are hyper-Calvinists who teach so, but they err by confusing predestination with *foreknowledge*. God foreknows everything (and has fore*told* some things) but that does not mean His having *predestinated* all that He foreknows or foretells. God never predetermined sin or any disobedience to His own will. Perish the thought! Sin and suffering belong to the lower level of His *permissive* will. All that God permits, however, He both anticipates and overrules. The millions of human beings who, during their earth-span, live outside God's particular plan for them, do so in His permissive will; but even the most rebellious of them cannot escape his all-controlling *governmental* will. There seem to be many professing Christians, too, who know little about living *in* and living *out* God's specific plan for them. Self-will frustrates its fulfilment. Our individual responsibility is to get into it, and then keep in it, through complete and continued consecration.

Another needed reminder is, that if we are to live out the plan carefully there must be *daily consultation* with Him who is *Master* of the plan in all its details. In a certain factory for the making of textile goods the instruction is: "If your threads get tangled, send for the foreman". A woman worker got her threads tangled and tried to disentangle them herself—only making them worse. After that she sent for the foreman. He asked, "Why did you not send for *me*, according to instructions?" Rather sullenly she replied, "I did my best". To this the foreman's rebuke was, "Always remember that 'doing your best' is *sending for me*". How often "doing our best" instead of consultation with the great Planner has badly tangled the threads!

So, let us grasp these big truths: (1) God has an advance purpose for each human life. (2) His purpose for us may be foiled by sin, as indeed occurs in numberless lives over which the God of John 3: 16 grieves. (3) In Christ, the restored, regenerated, consecrated Christian believer may really and fully implement that "pattern on the mount" (see again Eph. 2: 10, Phil. 2: 13). Let it be our deepest concern, then, to get into line with that divinely drawn plan, by an entire, continual, prayerful yieldedness to Christ. If we are young, let us be grateful to do so early. If we are older, let us remember that the "high calling" stretches on into the Beyond. Let us each pray it meaningfully: "Dear God, who hast a unique purpose and plan for *my* life, help me to get *into* it, and to *keep* in it, and to *fulfil* it, both here and hereafter".

> Thus to know Thy will and do it
> Let my high absorption be,
> Finding in Thy love and guidance
> Life unfettered, radiant, free.

PART TWO
ADJUNCTS OF GUIDANCE

Oh, to be always ready
    To do Thy perfect will ;
Alert for every challenge
    Thy purpose to fulfil !
Ready with verve and daring
    In holy war for Thee ;
Ready for burden-bearing,
    If that Thy will should be.

Oh, to be always ready
    To go or to abide,
A "vessel unto honour",
    "Prepared" and "sanctified" !
Ready for witness-bearing,
    Tho' stumbling, truly wise ;
Ready for sorrow-sharing,
    To soothe and sympathise.

Oh, to be always ready
    To serve without applause,
Forgiving, calm and steady,
    If blamed without a cause ;
Ready by daily lingerings
    In Thine own Word and prayer ;
Ready, at last, for heaven,
    To meet and serve Thee there.

                    J.S.B.

7

LIVING IN THE WILL OF GOD

BEYOND all doubt, and before all else, the experiencing of divine guidance in a human life is bound up with this supremely decisive matter of *living in the will of God*.

When Saul of Tarsus, the fanatically zealous Pharisee, was on his way to Damascus in fuming rage against the followers of the hated Nazarene, he was suddenly intercepted by the risen Lord Jesus. A blinding flash of light struck him to the earth, and he heard a voice asking, "Saul, Saul, why persecutest thou Me?" Trembling and astonished, he gasped, "Who art Thou, Lord?" and, "Lord, what wilt Thou have me to do?" Those two questions are the greatest any human being can ask, for they are more destiny-determining than all others.

First there is the question as to the *Person*: "Who art Thou, Lord?" As truly as He confronted Saul, so, in one way or another, Jesus confronts every other human being who knows about Him intelligently. He has been truly called "the inescapable Christ". He may be resented, evaded, accepted, rejected, but He cannot be escaped. That is because, in a way which affects and disturbs us all, He is the most mysterious and startling phenomenon of history.

Moses, Plato, Buddha, Mohammed, and all other notable religious originators, have been profoundly persuaded that they were pointing to realms of vital truth; and the more deeply they have felt this, so the more have they effaced themselves lest they should obtrude between their teaching and their hearers. Absolutely alone among leaders of the soul, Jesus absorbs all the highest principles of truth into His own personality and says, "*I AM* the Truth". In reply to the appeal, "Show us the Father," He says, "He that hath seen *ME* hath seen the Father." All the way through, with exquisitely blended humility and regality, His purpose—far more than expounding theological or ethical verities—is to *introduce HIMSELF* as our race's only Visitor from heaven; as "God manifest in the flesh"; as the One who alone gives forgiveness and soul-rest; as the one and only Saviour of the world.

"Never man spake like this Man" (John 7: 46). Never were such claims made by any other. Never was such sinless sublimity of character seen in any other. Never were such miracles performed by any other—crowned by His conquering of the very grave. Never was there expressed by any other teacher such knowledge of God, of man, of the future, of the beyond, of moral and spiritual truth. Never was there anywhere else such profound sympathy, compassion, self-sacrifice; such foreknown death and pre-avowal that it was to be an atonement for our sinful race.

Jesus is solitary, transcendent, unique, and in the deepest sense *incomparable*. He may be resisted, but He simply cannot be dismissed, however much men may think or pretend to have dismissed Him. Since Jesus came and spoke as He did, and lived as He did, and died as He did, and rose as He did, no atheist can be really comfortable; no agnostic can be truly at ease; no sceptic can sneer without subtle disquiet. This is confirmed by hundreds of them who have become converted and have then confessed that their prior attitudes were disguises to avoid *encounter* with Jesus.

Away back on that Damascus road, when the astonished future Apostle learned the true answer to his question, "Who art Thou, Lord?" his whole world was suddenly turned upside down—or, rather, right side up. So is it in every such vital encounter with Christ, however differing the outward circumstances. It is a soul-saving meeting with *GOD*; and the mind is fundamentally *converted*. Every aspect of life and things is changed by it. "Old things are passed away; behold all things are become new" (2 Cor. 5: 17). It revolutionizes our whole concept of God, of man, of morals, of the universe, of history, of life and death and the Beyond.

As soon as Saul, who now became Paul, had come into that earthquake discovery of the real *"LORD"*, there was only one thing which any more basically mattered. It was *"Lord, what wilt Thou have me to do?"* In other words, the vital thing is the risen Lord's will and purpose in a human life. The will of that risen Lord Jesus is the will of *God*. It is through that sin-atoning, death-vanquishing Redeemer and Reconciler that we each *get into* the direct will of God for us as human individuals. It is through our complete surrender to that dear Saviour, and through His unhindered control of us by the Holy Spirit, that the will of God is *in*wrought and then *out*wrought through us (Phil. 2: 13). That which the Spirit wills *in* us is that which the Son wills *for* us, and which the Father wills *through* us. The will of the Father and the Son and the Holy Spirit is the one will of God *for* us, and *in* us, and *through* us.

"Lord, what wilt Thou have me to do?" That is the supreme enquiry for each of us because it *includes* all else relating to our life-pattern. It is the most *far-reaching* of all questions, affecting the whole of our life, both here and hereafter. Apart from living in the *divine* will for me there can be no satisfying experience of God-guidedness; which means that life loses all its highest and most meaningful coherence. This is the really critical question—

AM I LIVING IN THE WILL OF GOD?

In Jesus (gracious mystery!) God comes to us making plainer than ever that His overall plan (including flowers as well as stars, and birds as well as angels) has a pre-mundane blueprint for every one of us individually. Think of God's word, centuries beforehand, spoken to the prophet Jeremiah,

"Before I formed thee . . . I knew thee; And before thou camest forth . . . I sanctified thee; I ordained thee a prophet unto the nations."

How that tender-hearted youth of little Anathoth must have wondered at it! And what sustenance it afforded him later amid permitted persecution and heart-break over the impenitence of Judah! He would ponder it again and again. Before ever he had come into actual being, he had existed in the anticipative purpose of God; and from his very birth he had been the subject of a pre-natal divine ordination! Or, think again of Paul's words in Galatians 1: 15,

"When it pleased God, who separated me from before my birth, and called me through His grace, to reveal His Son in me, that I might preach Him among the Gentiles, straightway I conferred not with flesh and blood."

Paul's word *"separated"* here does not refer to natural parturition, but to supernatural discrimination. Beyond doubt, the apostle is here teaching that before ever he drew his first baby breath there was a divinely fore-planned vocation for him.

But does such antenatal fore-intending pertain only to prophets and apostles? Does not the Word teach *antemundane* election of all true Christian believers into the mystic body and bride of Christ? Remember Ephesians 1: 4, "Chosen in Him before the foundation of the world"! Nor need we halt even there, for in John 9, when our Lord's disciples ask Him about the blind beggar, "Master, who did sin, this man, or his parents, that he was born blind?" our Lord's astonishing reply is, "Neither hath this man sinned, nor his parents; but [this is permitted] that the works of God should be made manifest in him"—whereupon Jesus gives the man sight; through which, also, he becomes a saved soul (9: 38). Which would you and I prefer?—to be born with sight but die spiritually blind like the proud Pharisees (9: 41); or to be born blind, then receive sight and become saved, like that one-time road-side beggar?

Christian believer, you may settle it in your mind: when you were born, not only were there present your mother, the doctor, the nurse, but angels, the Holy Spirit, and our dear Lord Himself —invisibly yet none the less personally present. Before ever your first baby cry fell on human ears, God foreknew you, and had a purpose for you. Does that seem almost unbelievably wonderful to you? Well, is it bearable (is it not torture) to think the opposite —that you are a microscopic accident of purposeless chance, or a meaningless dot in a vast blind fate?

Let Psalm 139 convince you that all your "members" were "written" in God's "book" before any of them took even embryonic form. Ever remember that God's basic relation to you, according to the Bible, is not creatorship or kingship or judgeship, but *fatherhood*. Did He create you just to be created?—or just to be ruled?—or just to be judged? No; He allowed you to be born because you are loved by Him. You are His *"child"*—born for loving fellowship and coöperative activity with Himself. His father-love covered you from *before* your birth, and *at* your birth; it covers you now, and will cover you to your last breath on earth; then on through that unfolding larger life in the mysterious Beyond.

The First Priority

All such considerations converge on this: that the first of all priorities for the Christian believer is to get into the direct line of that beneficial divine purpose. So, let us now consider briefly, but concentratedly, *living and serving inside the will of God*. Not only is this the concern of highest importance to every one of us; there surely cannot be any subject which strikes a more responsive chord in truly Christian hearts.

Paul's words about it in Romans 12: 2 may well claim our attention, though perhaps, if we would see its meaning more clearly, we should read it according to the marginal rendering of the American Standard Version, or, even better, as per Weymouth's *New Testament in Modern Speech*.

"Do not conform to the present age, but be transformed by the entire renewal of your minds, so that you may learn by experience what God's will is, namely all that is good and acceptable to Him and perfect."

So we are meant to *"learn by experience* what God's will is". We may know it and live in it. That focuses the whole matter for us. In the light of it let me submit a threefold way of thinking about living inside the will of God: (1) some urgent reasons for it, (2) some overlooked aspects of it, (3) some strange-seeming surprises about it.

Some Urgent Reasons

First, then, let me mention some urgent reasons. To begin with, inside the will of God is the only place of true *service*. There may be much religious activity outside the will of God, but it is not service. There may be much well-meaning, so-called Christian effort outside the will of God, but it is not service. There may be much good-quality preaching, much organizing, much church work, much evangelistic enterprise, outside the will of God, but it is not service. There may be much that is actually *called* "Christian service" outside the will of God, but it is not *really* service. That is because outside the accepted superintendence of God there is no divine guidance. Whatever is humanly self-managed is not divinely directed, and therefore cannot be truly service.

Again, inside the will of God is the only place of full *blessing*. I will not go so far as to say that outside of direct guidance there is *no* blessing, for God graciously accepts all well-meant labour in His Name, and often overrules it to good effect; but there cannot be *full* blessing, because it does not coincide in detail with the pre-designed pattern. Only when we are inside the will of God by complete yieldedness can we with certainty do just the right thing in just the right way at just the right time and with just the intended result.

Yet again, inside the will of God is the only place of rich *fellowship* with Him. Many Christian believers pray regularly, give generously, respond energetically, yet know little about secret, heart-to-heart conference with God, or about a deep, inward *enjoyment* of God through warm communion. The inward "Shekinah glow" of fellowship with the heavenly Father and with His Son Jesus Christ cannnot be known except by those who disallow anything to come between themselves and the will of God.

Looking back on earlier years, my beloved elderly friend, the late Professor John Henry Strong, tells a delightful little anecdote about D. L. Moody when that great evangelist was still in his prime. One day Moody heard a knock on his study door. "Come in," he said. His young son entered. "Well, my son, what is it you want?" "I don't want anything," came the answer, "but just to be with you." Oh, how many Christians there seem to be whose comings to God in prayer are little more than repeated applications to *get* something from Him! Their self-impoverished souls know nothing about that "just to *be with you*" longing of Moody's little son, or about the deep, utter joy of just being *with* God in secret fellowship. A father and his young son were on a journey and stayed overnight somewhere far from home. They occupied separate beds in the same room. "Son, you seem restless. Is anything troubling you?" The boy answered by asking, "Father, is your face turned toward me?" "Yes, my son." Without another sound the boy fell asleep. Nothing satisfies the true child of God like the loving look of the Father's face; and even if for that alone, being in the will of God means everything.

Still further, inside the will of God is the only place of indomitable *assurance*. When we are quite sure that we are filling a place or doing a work by clear divine guidance, then, whatever setbacks or oppositions there may be, we can weather them and surmount them with the strength of a realized divine approval. If we are *not* sure of being in the divine will, our hearts more quickly quail before recurrent discouragement. *Nothing* gives us courage, resilience, perseverance, like a deep love for Jesus and a certainty that we are in His will.

Once more, inside the will of God is the only place of utmost *self-fulfilment*. Since God alone knows us through and through—all our potentialities and all our future, none can guide and develop us as He can. He alone knows just what kind of place and service will effect for us a maximum fructifying of all that is best in our personalities. To have our *own* will and way often seems much freer and wider, but that is because we cannot see as far as God does. The most spacious of all true self-realization is inside our heavenly Father's plan for us. It gives to all we do the touch of immortality. Inside that will, nothing we do ever dies, for God is in it. Yes, that is the place of utmost self-fulfilment and, therefore, of fullest *satisfaction*.

Some Overlooked Aspects

But now let us notice certain aspects which some of us, at least, tend to overlook. For one thing, let none of us ever doubt that God's will covers the *non-religious* areas of our life. It is not limited to pulpits, mission stations, evangelistic campaigns, and other specifically Christian activities. Never since Paul has there been a greater missionary than William Carey, rightly called "the father of our modern missionary era"; but before ever that intrepid genius sailed from Britain for India he had learned to call himself, "William Carey, a cobbler by the will of God". During my ministry in Northampton, England, I occasionally visited the little cottage in the village of Moulton where young Carey used to live. What thoughts and feelings as I used to bend over the trough, still there, just inside the door, where he used to soak his leather! That shoe-making and cobbling business was as certainly a part of the divine design as was Carey's later high venture with the Gospel to India. As truly as Paul could designate himself "an apostle of Jesus Christ by the will of God", a Christian today may most definitely be a grocer, a banker, a clerk, a typist, a nurse, a housewife, "by the will of God".

Moreover, the will of God not only covers non-religious occupations in their general contour; it reaches right down to the hem stitches. To recount all the blessing which has come to human lives through Christian businessmen who conducted their businesses and their lives loyally within the will of God would run away with volumes. Their so-called "secular" vocations became their pulpits, and their lives were incarnate sermons!

Again, living in the will of God often means doing what we

love to do. Away for ever with the glum misprision that our heavenly Father's will seeks only to chain us to the galley oars of the hurtful or dislikeable! It is a *Father's* will, not a tyrant's! J. H. Jowett tells of a young woman who came to him asking, "Could you please tell me how to find God's will for my life?" Jowett learned that her mother was dead, her father was an invalid, and she, the young woman, looked after the invalid father. "Do you not think that God's will for you—at least for the present—is caring for your invalid father?" Jowett asked. Her reply was, "Well, sir, I can hardly think so. You see, I *love* doing that"!

How many there are who seem to have the subtle misconception that God begrudges our having the enjoyable! Some time ago I wandered through a cemetery which, as it had grown older and older, had grown larger and larger, until now it was one of the most expansive for many miles around. I became so interested in the differing types of gravestone inscriptions, especially between the older and the newer, that I asked a cemetery employee which was the commonest of them. He replied that the commonest two were, "Thy will be done" and "Rest in peace". It is nothing less than tragic that our idea of God's will should be so gloomily roped to the railings of the graveyard. Our yielding to God's will is never an interdict on joy: it is the gateway *to* it!

Very often, when we have to give something up in order to be in our Father's will, we get it back in sublimer form. One of my favourite novels is Charlotte Brontë's *Jane Eyre*. It seemed as though husbandly love would never come to plain Jane, but suddenly it did, in the person of a wealthy aristocrat. It was not love at first sight, but a heart-entwinement which soon grew into the real and lasting. The barrier was that Jane's wealthy lover was already married—to an incurably insane woman. The point of acute choice came. They could have each other, but only wrongly. At keen cost to all her tenderest feelings for the only lover she had known, Jane secretly fled far from the great house rather than disobey God's inner sentinel. It seemed as though by her own hand she was forever closing the door against her one and only hope of tangible happiness. But, as is often the case in human experience, Providence designed otherwise. Later we see the fine mansion destroyed by fire. Jane's lover incurs partial blindness and other injury in trying, unsuccessfully, to rescue his demented wife. Emerging from the ordeal, bereaved, disfigured, humbler and suddenly maturer, he now has a deep and aching *need* for Jane, who at last receives unexpected fulfilment of her fondest dreams in a lovelier, richer way; for gradually her husband largely recovers his sight, and their life together is such as belongs only to those who have loved and suffered for each other.

The story lives, not only by its literary gift, but because of its realism. It vividly illustrates what happens again and again when we faithfully adhere to the will of God. Instead of deprivation there is a richer fulfilment of holy desire than ever we had thought possible. See patriarch Abraham as he takes handsome young Isaac up Mount Moriah. The venerable old man would sooner lose even his inexpressibly precious Isaac than get out of the will of God. Then, just as the knife gleams in the sun, everything is changed: Abraham receives back, dearer than ever, that which he was willing to give up, and, along with it, one of the most staggering promises of blessing which God ever uttered to a man.

A further aspect is, that the will of God often expresses itself through our own *desires*. It has often been my privilege and responsibility to counsel young men and women concerning their careers. I remember how, in one instance, I had a distinct impression that one of my young men would make an excellent overseas missionary; but when I mentioned the matter to him he replied, "I feel pretty sure *that* cannot be God's will for me, because that is what I would *like* to be, more than anything else"! It would almost seem as though, if we *can* misjudge our heavenly Father's will, we are determined to do so! To those who really love Him, counting His will as "good and acceptable and perfect", He says through the psalmist, "Delight thyself in Jehovah, and He shall give thee the *desires* of thine heart." Indeed, when we are living in grateful yieldedness to Him, our most spontaneous desires are very often His first means of guiding us.

To this let us add one further word. Our ascertaining of God's will for us, whether for our career in general or for something only incidental, should be our *first* resort, not the *last*. One morning, when I was just a little boy, a neighbour called round on my Grandma to tell her that a sick woman down the lane was now in a serious condition. "Everything we could do has been done for her. There's nothing now but to leave her to the will of God." With commensurate gravity my grandma replied, "So it's come to that!" Perhaps the little incident is scarcely humorous enough to evoke a smile, yet it may well cause us to catch our breath, for that is how millions of us treat the will of God! We tinker about with a situation in confident self-wisdom, until, when we have made "confusion worse confounded" and we are at wit's end, we hand the havoc over to God as a last resort. Then, if divine guidance does not come at once to rescue us from our self-manipulated predicament, we wonder why God is so unconcerned!

We referred earlier to Weymouth's rendering of Romans 12: 2 —"That you may *learn by experience* what God's will is." In his footnote he suggests as an alternative: "That you may *habitually discriminate* what God's will is." Such continual perceiving of God's will through "entire *renewal*" of the *"mind"*, as indicated in Romans 12: 2, is so far removed from average Christian concept today that many are incredulous as to its possibility. But it is as real to God's Enochs amid the inane scramble of this twentieth century A.D. as it was in the leisurely decades before the Flood. I know men and women today who walk so closely with God that they experience this continual guidance. Theirs is the "joy unspeakable" and the "peace which passeth understanding". They have said a decisive "No" to the flesh, and a full "Yes" to God. Other than finding the will of God irksome their song is Faber's—

> I know not what it is to doubt,
>   My heart is always gay ;
> I run no risks, for, come what may,
>   He guards and guides my way.

In the years immediately following my conversion I used to pore over the diaries of the early Methodists. I find myself thinking again, just here, about the *Memoirs of William Carvosso*. That Cornish saint could not read or write till he was over fifty: but what a diary! In its way, it is a miniature classic of spiritual autobiography. How he walked with God! How consciously he walked in a continual recognition of the divine will! One of his favourite exclamations is, "Oh, the blessedness arising from a *heartfelt union* with a holy God!"

That "heartfelt union" is the essence of the serene joy which suffuses the hearts of all who, by consecration and habitual prayer and loving obedience, really live inside the heavenly Father's will. The love of God flooding the heart lifts it above envy and falsehood and pride ; above health-destroying tensions and the tumult of tormenting fears. Oh, that we all might grasp the truth of this, and act upon it!—for that is the place of long-coveted repose and peace and poise. Whatever the cost to self-aims, the highest of all wisdom is to get completely into the will of God. Years ago now, when my own slow-learning heart was struggling into a realization of this, my thoughts took shape in some lines which I will risk quoting; for I am even surer of their truth now than when I wrote them.

Dear Lord, I see it now so new and clear
Thy perfect will my highest good *must* be:
The yielding I have feared *removes all fear,*
For in Thy will where could I safer be?
Thou dost not wish to *break* this will of mine
That I a spineless negative should be,
But that my will should fondly partner Thine,
And all I am be harmonized with Thee.

Thou wouldst not have my will be *lost* in Thine,
But that with Thine it should be freely one;
Two wills, two minds, made one in love divine
Self-will (but not my true will) wholly gone:
My true, free-will *released* inside Thine own,
All egoistic, vain ambitions stilled,
Until with Thee I will one will alone
That *all* Thy best for me may be fulfilled.

Strange-Seeming Surprises

Finally, there is one other feature of living in God's will which must be mentioned, lest the inexperienced should be taken aback by strange-seeming surprises. Living in the will of God does not exempt us from *reverses.* That is because certain spiritual tutoring can come to us *only* that way. Such permitted reverses do not imply any suspension of guidance. They portend greater good.

Reverses? Yes. Do you think God's saintly Jobs, putting God first in everything, are not going to be eyed by the arch-fiend? Are we surprised that Satan determined on getting prayerful Daniel into the lions' den, and his three godly companions into the fiery furnace? They who will "stand perfect and complete in all the will of God" (Col. 4: 12) are bound to be an exasperation to the devil. He will devise stratagems to trick them, or upsets to jolt them out of the divine will, if he can. Job's reverses were such that it almost seemed as though God was mocking him; yet he came forth as "gold purified in the fire"; he inherited fuller blessing than ever, and became monumental for the rest of history!—

all because he would rather die than swerve from the will of God! The strange-seeming reverses which were permitted to fall upon Daniel, Shadrach, Meshach and Abed-nego were overruled to bring about the conversion of a world-emperor (Dan. 3: 28–30), and to spread the knowledge of the true God throughout all the Media-Persian world (6: 25–28).

Think again of William Carey. In the will of God? Most assuredly. Reverses? Enough to break the heart of any man. I mention just one. At the end of 1803 he wrote,

> "If we are given *another fifteen years* we hope to translate and print the Bible in all the chief languages of Hindustan. We have fixed our eyes on this goal. The zeal of the Lord of hosts will perform this."

Oh, the troubles, the dragging difficulties, the costliness of getting enough machine parts to assemble a printing press in that Calcutta compound! The slow, slow transit by sea! The scarcity of material! The cold discouragements from the British homeland! But dogged perseverance saw it accomplished! The translating and printing of Scripture and the Gospel began! How vital that printing press! The "zeal of the Lord of hosts" will surely protect it! No; not long afterward the whole of it goes up in flames! Oh, the stunning grief! *Why* has God permitted it? In a note to his nephew, Carey wrote,

> "I began this last night; I close it hastily this morning, having received intelligence of a dreadful loss, which befell the Mission last night. Our printing office was totally destroyed by fire, and all its property, amounting to at least Rs. 60,000 or 70,000. Nothing was saved but the presses. This is a heavy blow, as it will stop our printing the Scriptures for a long time. Twelve months' hard labour will not reinstate us; not to mention loss of property, MSS., etc., which we shall scarcely ever surmount. I wish to *be still, and know that the Lord is God,* and bow to His Will in everything. He will no doubt bring good out of this evil, and make it promote His interests; but at present the providence is exceeding dark. No lives were lost. We cannot tell what was the cause of the fire.
>
> > Your affectionate Uncle,
> > W. Carey."

Yet that calamity was astonishingly overruled. In the providence of God it was the news of that costly fire which suddenly turned the tide of feeling in Britain; so much so that Andrew Fuller wrote Carey,

"This fire has given your undertaking a celebrity which nothing else, it seems, could; a celebrity which makes me tremble. The public are now giving us their praises. Eight hundred guineas have been offered for Dr. Carey's likeness! If we inhale this incense, will not God withhold His blessing, and then where are we? Ought we not to tremble? Surely, all need more grace to go through good report than through evil."

Helpers suddenly appeared. Generous sums were donated. Far more was subscribed than had been lost. Permanent subscribing to the work multiplied. All kinds of printing improvements followed. And the song at Serampore was, "Our God hath turned the curse into a blessing" (Neh. 13: 2).

Perhaps, however, that which may seem strangest of all is, that living in the will of God does not always mean *success*—not, at least, in the sense of *earthly* success. Think of Adonira Judson, preaching the Gospel every day for fourteen years in a Burmese bazaar, without one convert. Think of Ezekiel: God says to him, "Son of man, go, get thee unto the house of Israel, and speak with My words unto them . . . But the house of Israel will *not* hearken unto thee." Then why send the prophet, if he is doomed to failure? Think of Jeremiah: if ever a man kept in the will of God, he did; yet instead of seeing his countrymen respond, he lived to see the crash of Jerusalem, and sat down amid the heart-rending ruins to weep his "Lamentations". Success? In the earthly sense, *No*. But in the will of God? *Yes*. Conscious of divine guidance? *Yes*. Sustained by the Holy Spirit? *Yes*. Joy amid tears? *Yes*. Wonderful fellowship with God? *Yes*. And a blessing to millions ever since, through their example and their prophecies? *YES*.

Oh, let it be said again: the only really safe place; the only place of unquenchable joy amid earthly flux and pathos; the only place of utmost self-fulfilment and benediction to others, is inside that fore-designed plan which God has for each of us. Of course, there is a sense in which *all* creatures—angel, demon, human, animal, sentient and non-sentient, are within the will of God; but

there is a vast difference between that *governmental* divine will
which none of us can *escape,* and the individualizing *fatherly* will
which each of us is meant to *fulfil.* Oh, to live inside that gracious
will all our earthly days, and to know the sense of God-guidedness
which accompanies it! The following lines were found among the
papers of an African missionary after his passing to the heavenly
homeland. What a consecration it expresses! God help us make
it the language of our own hearts!

Laid on Thine altar, O my Lord Divine,
    Accept my gift this day, for Jesus' sake ;
I have no jewels to adorn Thy shrine,
    Nor any world-famed sacrifice to make :
But here I bring within my trembling hands
    This will of mine, a thing that seemeth small,
Yet Thou alone, O Lord, canst understand
    How, when I yield Thee this, I yield Thee all :
Hidden therein, Thy searching gaze can see
    Struggles of passion, visions of delight,
All that I have, or fain would be,
    Deep loves, fond hopes, and longings infinite :
It hath been wet with tears, and dimmed with sighs,
    Clenched in my grasp till beauty it hath none :
Now from Thy footstool, where it vanquished lies,
    The prayer ascendeth, "May Thy will be done."
Take it, O Father, ere my courage fails,
    And merge it so in Thine own will that e'en
If in some desperate hour my cries prevail,
    And Thou give back my gift, it may have been
So changed, so purified, so fair have grown,
    So one with Thee, so filled with love Divine,
I may not know or feel it as my own,
    But gaining back my will, may find it Thine.

ABOUT SELF-MANAGEMENT

Only the very selfish or the very blind person is content to leave the world as it is today. Most of us would like to change the world.

The trouble is, too many of us want to do it our own way. Some people have the right diagnosis but they bring the wrong cure. They reckon without God and without a change in human nature, and the result is confusion, bitterness and war. Other people are quite sure they have the answer in theory, but they always want somebody else or some other nation to begin. The result is frustration and despair. When the right diagnosis and the right cure come together, the result is a miracle. Human nature changes and human society changes.

Let me illustrate this with a personal word, because it happened to me one day forty-four years ago. For the first time I saw myself with all my pride, my selfishness, my failure and my sin. "I" was the centre of my own life. If I was to be different, then that big "I" had to be crossed out.

I saw the resentments I had against six men standing out like tombstones in my heart.

I asked God to change me, and He told me to put things right with those six men. I obeyed God and wrote six letters of apology.

That same day God used me to change another man's life. I saw that when I obeyed God miracles happened. I learnt the truth that when man listens, God speaks; when man obeys, God acts; when men change, nations change.

Frank Buchman.

8

ABOUT SELF-MANAGEMENT

MOST of us who somehow fail to live in God's specific will for us do not stay outside it through wilful rebellion, but because we succumb to the lure of self-management. We fall into the snare of which Paul warns us in Galatians 3: 3, "Are ye so foolish? having begun in the Spirit, are ye now made perfect by the flesh?"

We Christian believers certainly *did* "begin in the Spirit". It was He who first wrought within us to convict us of our sin, to convince us of our need, and to convert us to the Saviour. It was He who effected within us our spiritual rebirth, infusing the new life which regenerated us. Of sheer necessity, in a spiritual sense, we *live* in the Spirit. Therefore it is utterly consistent for Paul to exhort us in Galatians 5: 25, "If we *live* in the Spirit, let us also *walk* in the Spirit."

Alas, the contradictory anomaly is, that many of us who in this regenerating sense "live" in the Spirit only *partly* "walk" in the Spirit. Without sensing the foolish self-delusion of it we secretly assume that we can manage our spiritual life better than the One who imparted it to us! We do not reason this out (we could not even if we tried, for there is no "reason" in it); we simply assume it, in our inborn natural egoism. Almost unthinkingly, but at the cost of pathetic spiritual stuntedness, we "walk in the flesh", i.e. according to our own self-centred natural wisdom, desires, and urges.[1]

But besides engendering spiritual immaturity and deformity, this "taking things into our own hands" and living by self-management (or *mis*-management) is responsible more than anything else for tricking us into painful situations and inflicting hurtful sorrows upon us. How many examples of this there are in the pages of Holy Writ! I have often said that the most telling illustrations of New Testament doctrine are found in Old Testament story;

---

[1] For a full treatment of that phrase, "the flesh", in its figurative usage, see our volume, *A New Call to Holiness*.

and it is certainly true in this connection. It may well serve as a wise warning to some of us if we here pick out just a few of those Old Testament episodes which say to us, "Are ye so foolish? Having begun in the Spirit, are ye now made perfect by the flesh?"

Abram goes to Egypt

The first such instance which leaps to mind is that of Abram's going down into Egypt, as recorded in Genesis 12: 10–20. Run through the short passage again.

> "There was a famine in the land: and Abram went down into Egypt to sojourn there; for the famine was grievous in the land. And it came to pass, when he was come near to enter into Egypt, that he said unto Sarai his wife: Behold now, I know that thou art a fair woman to look upon; therefore it shall come to pass, when the Egyptians shall see thee, that they shall say, This is his wife; and they will kill me, but they will save thee alive. Say, I pray thee, thou art my sister; that it may be well with me for thy sake; and my soul shall live because of thee. And it came to pass that when Abram was come into Egypt, the Egyptians beheld the woman that she was very fair. The princes also of Pharaoh saw her, and commended her before Pharaoh; and the woman was taken into Pharaoh's house. And he entreated Abram well for her sake: and he had sheep, and oxen, and he asses, and menservants, and she asses, and camels. And the Lord plagued Pharaoh and his house with great plagues because of Sarai, Abram's wife. And Pharaoh called Abram, and said, What is this that thou hast done unto me? Why didst thou not tell me that she was thy wife? Why saidst thou, She is my sister? so I might have taken her to me to wife. Now therefore behold thy wife, take her, and go thy way. And Pharaoh commanded his men concerning him: and they sent him away, and his wife, and all that he had."

We can make sympathetic allowance for the circumstances which caused Abram to decide on going down into Egypt; yet his doing so was wrong. There seems to have been no waiting on God about it. Instead of seeking divine direction, he took the matter into his own hands. Indeed, his going down into Egypt seemed so obviously the thing to do that perhaps he never even thought to consult higher wisdom.

See, now, what happens. Abram suddenly realizes in a new way what a beautiful woman his wife is. Hitherto he has taken Sarai pretty much for granted, but as soon as he seems likely to lose her he realizes what a precious treasure she is to him, and how desirable she is. (Many a husband fails to realize what a priceless treasure his wife is until he comes to lose her! Many of us fail to value blessings which are ours until they are removed. We may well prize them while we have them.)

Abram makes a compact with Sarai to have her say she is his sister. It was a shifty expedient, even though she *was* his half-sister; and it resulted in a frightening development. The Egyptian pharaoh coveted Sarai, whereupon, believing she was Abram's unmarried sister, he "entreated Abram well" for her, and had her taken into his house. Witness the tragic predicament into which Abram has brought both of them. Here is Sarai, the woman who was destined to be the mother of the miracle-babe, Isaac, in whom all the divine promises were wrapped up for the coming of the Messiah-Redeemer and the blessing of all kindreds of the earth—here she is, the prospective mother of the Seed Royal, in the harem of an Egyptian pharaoh!

Yes, that is what has happened through Abram's leaning to his own natural wisdom. His beloved and beautiful Sarai in dire jeopardy, and the Messianic promises imperilled! Had it not been that God Himself intervened, His far-reaching purposes through Abram would have been aborted there and then.

We agree again that the circumstances which led Abram to go down into Egypt were pressing. He was only doing what Bedouin tribes have done right down until recent times, in similar circumstances. We can also make sympathetic allowance for Abram's fears about his own safety as Sarai's husband. In the British Museum there is an ancient papyrus which, although of rather later date than Abram, proves that his fears were not groundless. It tells how a pharaoh, on the advice of his counsellors, sent armies to take away a man's wife and to murder her husband.

Yes, we make allowance for *all* of that; yet Abram's action was wrong. It was of the flesh, not of the Spirit. It was the contrivance of human wisdom; not divine guidance. There was purpose in the famine which God had permitted to overspread the

land of Canaan. God purposed to teach Abraham that even in
the "land of promise", in the place of covenanted blessing, nourish-
ment and prosperity depended on walking with God day by day,
i.e. on "walking in the Spirit".

Ishmael and Isaac

Years later, sadly enough, Abram gives us another example of
the same thing, for this slipping back into walking "after the
flesh" is always perilously easy. God had given the childless
Abram a promise that he should yet have a son of his own (Gen.
15: 4). Years slip away; still no sign of the promised heir. Abram
is now eighty-five and Sarai seventy-five. God must have forgotten His promise, or He is strangely dilatory. The ten years
with no sign of fulfilment prove too much for Sarai. She decides
that God needs helping on a bit, before it is too late. Presumably
she herself cannot now bear Abram a son; and there are times
when he cannot disguise his deep disappointment. So something
must be done at this point (says self-wisdom). Somehow Sarai
manages to talk Abram into agreeing. The result is that Abram
has a son!—but not of Sarai.

Now see what follows. That which Sarai presupposed would be
a clever success proves to be her most cutting regret. Hagar, the
proud mother of Ishmael, but still maid to Sarai, *despises* her
mistress until the intolerable friction between two jealous women
wears away all peace from Abram's dwelling. Ishmael inherits
the truant nature of his Egyptian mother; yet naturally Abram
loves him—loves him dearly as his one and only child; loves
him so much, in fact, that when God announces, thirteen years
later, the impending birth of a son through Sarai, the patriarch
entreats, "Oh, that *Ishmael* might live before thee!" Isaac is born,
is weaned, and grows through childhood. Ishmael resents and
mocks him. In the words of Galatians 4: 29, "He that was born
of the *flesh* persecuted him that was born after the *Spirit*."

Soon, under Abram's roof, an ugly crisis develops between the
two mothers and their two sons. Sarah, whose clever self-wisdom
was the genesis of all the trouble, demands that the slave-woman
and her son be driven out. God now intervenes, lest harm should
come to little Isaac, and tells Abraham to do as Sarah demands.
With heartbreak and tears Abraham sees his beloved Ishmael
expelled—sees him for the last time. As for that wild young colt,
the expulsion deepens his hate toward Isaac. He has felt it ever

since. It has lasted nearly four thousand years. This very day we are seeing new expression of it in the Middle East. It was Ishmael's progeny who followed Mohammed and became the fanatical sword-bearers of Islam. It was the Mohammedans who captured Jerusalem about 600 A.D. and have fiercely held it until present times. It is they who, more malignantly than all others, have resisted Christian missionary witness in different parts of the world. It is they who, at this very hour, are crying death to the new Israeli State in Palestine. The world is still reaping tragedy because, long ago, Sarah and Abraham took things out of God's hands, and "walked after the flesh"!

David Among the Philistines

Take a long leap from patriarch Abraham to royal David. In outstanding ways David is exemplary as a man of faith in God. Above all else he wanted to walk in the will of Israel's God, and to follow sure pointers of guidance at every step. Yet in David, also, we see long-regretted lapses into this "walking after the flesh". Glance at just one of them, recorded in I Samuel 27: 1–7.

"And David said in his heart, I shall now perish one day by the hand of Saul: there is nothing better for me than that I should speedily escape into the land of the Philistines; and Saul shall despair of me, to seek me any more in any coast of Israel: so I shall escape out of his hand. And David arose, and he passed over with the six hundred men that were with him unto Achish, the son of Maoch, King of Gath. And David dwelt with Achish at Gath, he and his men, every man with his household, even David with his two wives, Ahinoam the Jezreelitess, and Abigail the Carmelitess, Nabal's wife. And it was told Saul that David was fled to Gath: and he sought no more again for him. And David said unto Achish, 'If I have now found grace in thine eyes, let them give me a place in some town in the country, that I may dwell there: for why should thy servant dwell in the royal city with thee?' Then Achish gave him Ziklag that day. And the time that David dwelt in the country of the Philistines was a full year and four months."

This sudden wilting of David's trust is not without some strange-ness. He knew that God had anointed him to succeed Saul as king, and he was content to wait God's time. He knew that God had enabled him to slay the lion and the bear—and even Goliath. He knew that Jonathan, Saul's son and natural heir, was his own utterly loyal friend, and that Jonathan magnanimously rejoiced in David's divine appointment to the throne. Why, then, should David now compromise himself by fleeing for shelter among Israel's sworn enemies, the Philistines?

Hunted like a "partridge on the mountains", his spirit had become worn down through Saul's insensate pursuit of him. Ten times now, in all, Saul had sought to kill him. How long must the hunt go on? How long must David dart from one precarious hideout to another? Faith suddenly cracks: "I shall perish one day by the hand of Saul"! That is just the opportunity for self-management to swing into play. Self-wisdom at once says, "The commonsense thing is to put yourself beyond his reach—which you can easily do by crossing the border for a time." Forgetting to seek counsel at the Mercy Seat, David takes things into his own hands, and goes. It was understandable (it always is) but it was wrong.

See how David is forced to compromise and entangle himself. Somehow he must first convince Achish, king of Gath, that he has finally split from Israel. This he does by brazen lying and by slaughtering the inhabitants of various cities, pretending to Achish that he was slaying Israelites! Then, when the Philistines make war against Israel, David finds himself in the fearful predicament of having to go with them! The very one who had been anointed by Jehovah to take the throne of the covenant people, after Saul, now going up with Israel's worst enemies to fight against his own throne and kingdom, and, thereby, against his own God! By a providential intervention David was prevented from going into battle against his own countrymen; but (not to mention other self-inflicted frustrations) after Saul's death eleven out of Israel's twelve tribes *refuse* David, and there is a full seven years of delay before he becomes king. Yes, the "wisdom of the flesh" can be very costly!

Elimelech Goes to Moab

Let me pick out just one further Old Testament incident which illustrates how things go wrong when we act in fleshly wisdom instead of waiting for and abiding in the revealed will of God. In the Book of Ruth, that redeeming little addendum to the Book of Judges, chapter 1: 1–5, we read:

"Now it came to pass in the days when the judges ruled, that there was a famine in the land. And a certain man of Bethlehem-Judah went to sojourn in the country of Moab, he, and his wife, and his two sons. And the name of the man was Elimelech, and the name of his wife Naomi, and the name of his two sons Mahlon and Chilion, Ephrathites of Bethlehem-Judah. And they came into the country of Moab, and continued there. But Elimelech, Naomi's husband, died; and she was left, and her two sons. And they took them wives of the women of Moab: the name of the one was Orpah, and the name of the other Ruth: and they dwelled there about ten years. And Mahlon and Chilion died also, both of them; and the woman was left without her two sons and her husband."

As elsewhere, so in this instance, the circumstances which pro-voke acting in "the flesh" are understandable: "famine in the land." But did that Israelite do right in forsaking the place of promised blessing to live in alien territory and amid idolatry with his wife and family? Perhaps, in modern jargon, he reasoned that "keeping soul and body together" came before even "religion". At any rate, he left Bethlehem for Moab.

The name Bethlehem means "House of Bread" (*Beyth* = house; *lechem* = bread). The name of Elimelech means, "God is my King" (Eli = God; melech = king). His wife's name, Naomi, means *sweetness*. The names of their two sons, Mahlon and Chilion, mean, if anything, *mildness* and *completeness*.[1]

What happens in Moab? Elimelech ("God is my King") dies. So do Mahlon and Chilion ("mildness" and "completeness"). After ten tragic years Naomi, the pathetic remnant, returns to Bethlehem, but instead of her being any longer "Naomi" (sweet-ness), she gives herself a new name: "Call me not Naomi but *Mara* [*bitter*]." How often, when we resort to the expedients of self-wisdom instead of abiding in God's will we lose our sense of "God is my King" (Elimelech); and bereave ourselves of life's truest heart-comforts (our Mahlons and Chilions); and eventually come back sadly sighing, "*Mara*" (bitter)!

Besides the foregoing, other such instances might easily be given from the pages of Holy Writ, exhibiting in one way or another the harvests of regret which grow from our sowings in

---

[1] See note by Dr. James Morison in Pulpit Commentary.

the self-sure "wisdom of the flesh". Either by direct word or by some telling illustration the Scriptures touch on it again and again, to deter us from it, and to educate us in the superior wisdom which puts God first in every choice, larger or lesser. Without lingering over them, we think of illustrations such as Moses' two efforts to rescue Israel from Egyptian tyranny—the first time in "the flesh" when he was forty, which resulted in murder, flight, and forty years of delay; the second time in the direct will of God, which brought about one of the mightiest deliverances in history.

Or we think of Israel's clamour for a human king. Through Samuel God faithfully forewarned them of the eventualities, but they presumed to know better. They were unanimous that the glitter of a visible crown and throne and sceptre would greatly enhance the prestige of the nation. So they had their own way—with a brilliant beginning in the handsome young Saul; but oh, what disruptive and punishing after-effects lasting to this very day!

Or again we think of impulsive Simon Peter's "I go a fishing", in John 21, and the responsive, "We also go with thee" of the other six. Soon the newly floated company with managing-director Peter are "in business", but by morning, despite wearying expenditure, they are bankrupt—"that night they caught nothing"! How impulsively they had started ("they entered into a ship *immediately*")! And what a risk they were taking! Satan would with fiendish satisfaction have sunk that little boat, for its seven occupants had in their possession redeeming facts sufficient to "turn the world upside down" and to save millions of human souls for ever! How they show us, all unwittingly, that in service for our risen Lord prayerless *rush* is always foolish *risk*! But see what happens when morning comes. The voice of Jesus rings out across the water, "Cast the net on the right side of the ship, and ye shall find." And now *Christ*-directed service transforms everything! Oh, that all of us, as the Lord's servants, might "read, mark, learn, and inwardly digest"!

Even the Spirit-filled Pauls need to keep on guard against sidestepping into "the flesh". Twice, in Acts 21, we find the Holy Spirit warning Paul not to go to Jerusalem at that time (verses 4 and 11). Yet Paul went. Apparently he reasoned that without delay he ought to carry the gifts from the Gentile churches of Macedonia and Achaia to the needy believers over in Judea (Rom. 15: 25–29). Paul's guidance up to that point was that he must go to *Rome* (Acts 19: 21 with 23: 11 and 27: 24). It would seem that he himself interposed Jerusalem. The dire results we well know. Had it not been for supernatural preservation, Paul would have been lynched by the frenzied mob at Jerusalem, and would never have seen Rome at all. We all admire Paul's lofty bravery: "I am ready not only to be bound but also to die at Jerusalem for the name of the Lord Jesus." Yet even such splendid valour as that is no warrant to step outside God's revealed will; for whenever we do so, we involve *others* as well as penalizing ourselves.

Sources of Temptation

What should be our reaction to these recurrent red lamps of warning in Scripture? Well, if we would live in the experience of continual God-guidedness, the big question is: How may we learn to overcome this ever-present proneness to slip outside the divine will into self-management? In reply I would earnestly recommend: School yourself in recognizing the *sources* of temptation to it. I think the three main sources are (1) permitted testings, (2) divine silences, (3) irritating circumstances; and I offer three corresponding counsels.

First, be alert to *permitted testings*. God never tempts any man (Jas. 1: 13), but He does allow us to be tested. This has been true from Adam downwards. In the very nature of things it is inevitable that it should be so; for only thus, in this school of our earthly life, can we graduate in the "higher education" of the soul. Comparatively seldom (so I believe) does God *impose* such tests. Far more generally He simply *permits* them through the natural sequence of happenings. Occasionally, too, He permits Satan to try us (Job 1: 12, Luke 22: 31 A.S.V. margin), but always in such instances He sets a firm limit (1 Cor. 10: 13).

Never allow any foothold to the thought that being tried is being tricked. The whole Bible is God's pledge to us that in being tried we are being *trained*. Often we must be tested by bruising before we can be trusted with blessing. There are no "quick and easy" methods in the reproducing of the divine image in human character. Some friends of ours had a precocious little son. He was also history's slickest little thief of candies. What was amusing at first assumed a more serious complexion later, for there seemed to be an abnormal craving creating intentional dishonesty. One morning his mother said to us, "We've cured him, but it's taken patient lessons and some hard tests. Sometimes we've hidden and then watched him—though we felt pretty mean in doing so. We've seen him drooling at the very sight of those tempting candies, but he won a thorough victory. This morning he said to me, 'Mommie, I love you so much: *I'd sooner please you* than eat twenty Riley's bon-bons'."[1] It is a great day in the soul's tuition when at last we would rather please God than let *anything,* however attractive, allure us out of His will. If there have to be testings to get us there, we must keep our eyes on the "nevertheless afterward" (Heb. 12: 11) of reward. Let us never think testings are cruel. The God who bled on Calvary can never mock us with a needless trial.

Wait it Out

Again, we would counsel: Learn to wait during *divine silences.* It has been truly said that "the silence of God is the severest test of faith". There are divine silences which seem unreasonable, even to the point of being unbearable. Some of the psalmists knew that problem: "Why standest Thou afar off, O Lord? Why hidest Thou Thyself in times of trouble?" (10: 1). "O Lord my rock, be not silent to me, lest, if Thou be silent to me, I become like them that go down into the pit" (28: 1). See also psalms 35: 22, 83: 1. Such silences easily induce the helpless feeling within us that God is apathetic or deaf as ancient Baal. "Hope deferred maketh the heart sick" (Prov. 13: 12). We succumb to faintness of heart (Luke 18: 1), which is just the point of human weakness at which we capitulate to circumstance and act at self-dictation.

That is just how king Saul, long ago, first side-stepped the will of God. The prophet Samuel had told Saul to wait for him seven days. As the seventh day began to wear away, Saul, who was in seemingly desperate straits, acted; and in doing what he thought was right he did the thing that was wrong. If only he had waited another half-hour Samuel would have been there with God's answer. The delaying of answer was not that God was tantalizing Saul; the only way to prove him and develop him spiritually was an acute time-test. That the test was needed is shown by Saul's later behaviour; for it was his impulsive self-will which caused his spiritual disintegration.

We should not leave this aspect of divine guidance unstudied

---

[1] A favourite English toffee.

until some stiff experience of it is permitted. We should deliberately encounter it, and think it through while we are still un-
pressured. This will fortify us in advance. Let us accept it as a
part of our spiritual education: and let us be firmly convinced
that divine silences *always* have some beneficial design in them.
Thus forearmed, we shall endure, and eventually find ourselves
singing with the same psalmist who wondered why God was
silent: "I *waited patiently* for the Lord . . . and He hath put a
new song in my mouth" (Ps. 40: 1–3). Remember: God says,
"They shall not be ashamed that *wait* for Me" (Isa. 49: 23).

Misreading of Circumstances

Another source of temptation to take things into our own hands
is our misreading of *obstinate circumstances*. Like Jacob of old,
we lament, "Joseph is not, and Simeon is not, and ye will take
Benjamin away: all these things are against me!" (Gen. 42: 36).
Poor, harassed old Jacob! We can understand his gush of grief.
Yet had he only known it, the scowling appearance of things
was being utterly misjudged. The very transpirings which seemed
to scourge him were paving the way to the loveliest of sequels.
Soon, now, he would be exclaiming, "Joseph, my son, is yet
alive!" A judgment of God's dealings which is based on one particular trial is seldom true. Often God's choicest purposes of blessing wind to their consummation through strange-seeming permis-
sions. Hear William Cowper again—

> Judge not the Lord by feeble sense ;
>   Still trust His sovereign grace ;
> Behind each frowning providence
>   He hides a smiling face.

There are times when it is so *easy* to misjudge the appearance
of things that the above stanza can seem uncomforting: yet few
of us have had to bear what the poet Cowper had—and his song
of confidence was a product of proving God through permitted
trouble!

Years ago, someone gave me a little tract by Grace Leonora
Klahr. Let me here quote from it. "Sometimes we have our hearts
set upon attaining a certain object but God has something better
for us, and has to hedge up our way so that we will not go in
the wrong direction. We, in our blindness, cannot understand
why our way is so hedged about, and may be tempted to cry

out in bitterness of soul with Jeremiah, 'He hath hedged me about, that I cannot get out: he hath made my chain heavy' (Lam. 3: 7). Some years ago the following incident was related by a returned missionary from Africa. One day after the missionaries had finished their noon meal, one of the lady workers noticed that her child was chewing something. The others gave it no thought, but the mother felt anxious to determine what it was; so she went into an adjoining room. A moment later they heard her scream. The child had found the calomel and had evidently taken about 25 grains—much more than enough to cause its death. They were in central Africa and many days' journey from a doctor. The mother flung herself down beseeching the Lord to spare the child. They searched the doctor books and found the invariable antidote to be the white of an egg. It is only at certain seasons of the year that they are able to secure eggs there, and this was the season when they were getting none. The little one expressed a desire to go to sleep, which was certain evidence that the drug was taking effect. As they continued to pray, a native appeared at the door and in his hand was—an egg! They hastily broke it open and found to their grief that it was bad! They were tempted to feel mocked in their cries for help, but they renewed their pleading. Soon another native appeared at the door with a dozen fresh eggs! They gave the child one of the whites which proved an effective emetic, and in three days the little one was normal again."

Not often, but occasionally, as in the foregoing incident, something may be permitted which could seem even to mock our appeal to God. It *can* be a stratagem of Satan to strain our trust to breaking point, to incite resentment, or to induce a gloom of futility. Oh, at that point, how easy it is to misinterpret the swing of the pendulum, and act independently of God! At such times we may feel as Moses did, away back yonder in his first encounter with Pharaoh. He was certain, up to that point, of being in the line of divine guidance; and with a ring of confidence in his tones he told Pharaoh, in the name of Jehovah, that he must now let the Hebrews leave Egypt. Instead of compliance there was sarcastic defiance—"Who is this Jehovah?" Next there is angry retaliation from the Egyptian throne, and the already suffering Hebrews are subjected to even harsher rigours. With less materials they must achieve more result. Harried, driven, flogged, exhausted, the Hebrews groan more than ever, and Moses flings himself down before God, protesting: "Lord, wherefore hast Thou so evil entreated this people? why is it that Thou hast sent me? For since I came to Pharaoh, to speak in Thy name, he hath done evil to this people; neither hast Thou delivered Thy people at all" (Exod. 5: 22, 23). Had Moses only realized it, the defiant refusal by Pharaoh was the gateway to such a mighty deliverance of Israel, and such a revelation of the true God, that history has talked of it ever since.

Each of us may well be on the *qui vive* against deceptive *appearances*. Too often, in my own experience, when I have been seeking special guidance in problematical matters, I have too readily misinterpreted some turn of circumstance, and under a shadow of unbelief have inferred that instead of an answer God had sent an irritation!—only to find at the *next* "turn" that I had mistaken a herald of kindness for an opponent!

A ship was wrecked. There was one lone survivor. He was washed on to a small, uninhabited island. In his extremity he cried urgently for God to save him, and daily scanned the horizon to catch sight of any ship. He managed to build a rough hut in which to put the few articles which he had salvaged from the wreck. One day, after searching for food, he was stunned with grief to find the hut going up in flames and smoke. Soon it was gone. The worst had happened. What an answer to prayer! Early next day a ship drew in. When the marooned man asked the captain what had caused him to come, the captain replied, *"We saw your smoke signal!"*

Dear Christian: school your mind in William Cowper's classroom! Learn it fixedly that behind "frowning providences" is your heavenly Father's sympathetic watchfulness. Beware of hastily misreading strange-seeming shifts of circumstance when you are sincerely committing a situation to God. Let Jacob's "all these things are against me" be your warning, not your example!

A Sheaf of Advice

In conclusion, here is a sheaf of short but pertinent recommendations.

First, do not let delayed answer in *one* matter blind you to the divine guidance that is going on all the time in all the other matters which concern you. Delay in one does not mean suspension of all.

Second, stimulate your patience by reflecting that very often the longer the wait the bigger the answer. What an illustration of this is Joseph! What a wait!—and through what black discouragements! but what a sequel!

Third, keep reminding yourself that through many a delay-process God is trying to teach us something which may be better even than the answer we are wanting.

Fourth, despite aggravation to act hastily in any critical situation be assured that in the end God's delays save more time than man's hurry, and achieve results with no regrets.

Fifth, let Scripture and experience alike testify to you, that nearly always delayed answers and waiting periods lead to bigger discovery of God, and greater glory to His name.

Sixth, if kept waiting, remember Matthew 7: 7, "Ask, and it shall be given to you; seek, and ye shall find; knock, and it shall be opened to you." The second part of that text is in participles: "For every one who is *asking* receives, and he who is *seeking* finds, and to him who is *knocking* it shall be opened." So it is not just *one* "ask", one "seek", one "knock"! Keep *on* asking; keep *on* seeking; keep *on* knocking!

Seventh, guard against dictating that prayer must be answered *your* way. What *you* are sure is either the best or even the *only* way may be *far* from that. I put on record my thanks to God for the times He has said "No"—and sent something far better than I asked. Lord, save us from prayerless self-management! Lord, save us from taking things into our own hands! Having "begun in the Spirit", may we not think to be "made perfect by the flesh". Keep us watchful against the *sources* of temptation to stride outside Thy will. Give us the "faith and *patience* of the saints" in times when we are kept waiting.

PRAYER AND GUIDANCE

He [Dr. Oswald J. Smith] has lived missions, he has preached missions, he has written missions, he has supported missions. . . . Under his leadership the Peoples Church in Toronto has raised more than $5,000,000 for missions . . . and the total from all sources . . . reaches the astronomical $12,000,000.

One day, on entering the lounge of an hotel in Chicago, the writer saw Mrs. Smith, sitting in a corner. . . . I asked her where her husband was. "He's up in our room," she replied. "He's praying, and he walks while he prays. There isn't room for me in there. So I leave him to pray alone."

Walking while praying. The phrasing is apt. These two aspects of the spiritual life must always go together.

Douglas C. Percy,
in *Evangelical Christian.*

9

PRAYER AND GUIDANCE

A PRAYERLESS life can never be a God-guided life. That may seem too obvious to need saying; but it is one of those axioms which, despite their self-evident truth, need often repeating, so slow are we to act on them. Because of its varied facets and bearings prayer is a fascinating subject. In one sense nothing could be simpler.

> "Prayer is the simplest form of speech
> Which infant lips can try."

Yet in its relation to the providential government of the world, and the universality of natural law, its operation is mysterious and profound.

Into the theological and speculative aspects of prayer we neither need nor purpose to enter here. We are concerned solely with its *practical* pertinence in the Christian life, particularly as relates to divine guidance.

Deep in our hearts, all of us *know* that nothing is more vital to our spiritual development than prayer; that without it there cannot be fellowship with God, power for effective Christian witness, holiness of character, or any continuing divine guidance in our life. Yet most of us live in chronic apology and regret that we pray so little.

> Oh, strangest failure one can tell,
> I know my need of prayer so well,
> And I would often be in prayer,
> Yet somehow little time can spare!
>
> I ought to pray for very fear
> Of snares and dangers ever near—
> A world without, a foe within,
> A tempter who disguises sin!
>
> I ought to pray for very love
> Of Him who listens from above—
> My secret interview with Christ
> The ever-longed-for daily tryst!

I ought to pray for very bliss
At such a privilege as this—
My Saviour gives to all His own
A blood-bought access to the Throne!

I "ought"—oh, let me say, "I will",
And daily my high pledge fulfil;
Until, by frequent lingerings there,
My heart becomes a *"house* of prayer".

Why is it, that although we recognise the vital role of prayer, so many of us neglect it? Reasons are not far to seek. The first is a natural sluggishness against which we all have to contend. One of the most effective ways to overcome this is to admit it and squarely face it. To keep disguising it rather than concede to ourselves that we are naturally "unspiritual", does not help; it hinders. That combine of hereditary, self-centred dispositions in us which Paul sums up as "the flesh" just does not "take" to regular prayer. To "the flesh" prayer seems unpractical, tedious, a pious waste of time which could be used more expeditiously in other ways to "get things moving". Thus, although the new life of the Spirit within us cries out for prayer, there is all the while that unrelenting drag-away of "the flesh".

Besides this, prayer is that spiritual exercise which above all else *Satan opposes*. As the king of Syria, long ago, commanded his captains to "fight neither with small nor great, but only with the king of Israel" (1 Kings 22: 31), so do the powers of darkness concentrate all the force of their opposition against the spirit of prayer; for they know that believing prayer in the name of Jesus is the most potent apparatus committed to the Christian Church and its members. Satan grasps, far more astutely than most of ourselves do, that in the economy of redemption prayer creates a channel for the release of divine power,to save men and defeat evil, which otherwise there would not be. He knows that every major visitation of spiritual revival in the history of the organized Church has come in answer to the travailing prayer of the saints. He knows just as vividly that the habit of regular, lingering prayer, more than anything else, makes any Christian a dangerously holy weapon in the hand of God.

Another major detriment to regular prayer nowadays is the *pitch and tempo* of modern life. Our predecessors lived by the sun-dial and the calendar. We gadget-encircled beneficiaries of the science era live by the alarm clock. Those time-saving, labour-saving wheels and wonders which were going to smooth human life into new leisure have somehow rolled twice as much to do into half the time to do it, until for millions in our crowded cities nearly all lilt and poise in life are gone! For many the usual day is a non-stop "doing the next thing next", always to a deadline, until leisure seems a far-off foreign shore. This creates two problems in relation to habitual prayer: (1) the difficulty of finding a daily period immune from invasion, (2) the stilling of minds which have become galvanized into chronic hurry.

Well, those are some of the reasons why the path of prayer is irregularly trodden. Is there any effective counter to them? Let me mention here at least *one* which has had decisive value for myself. After much dreary experience in what has been called "the barrenness of an overcrowded life", I reached a point of self-encounter at which I deliberately compelled myself to survey my prayerless scramble objectively enough to find out once for all what was causing the dismal spiritual failure. I asked myself: What are life's *supremes*?—the "first priorities" to live for? Answers soon came, and I let them burn into my thinking for the rest of my years on earth.

I asked myself: Which comes first, religious service?—or knowing *God*? Which has the *basic* importance: what I do?—or what I *am*? Which means more, both to God and men: quantity? —or *quality*? Which means more to Christ: my work for Him? —or my prayerful *love* for Him? In Christian life and service, which is the *utterly* vital: ability, activity?—or inwrought holiness of character? What would my reactions be about all these things (I asked myself) when at last I should meet my heavenly Master? Would I be meeting a Master whom I recognised by His incomparable splendour, but did not know personally (having been too busy serving)?—or would I at last be meeting face to face One whom I had for years known heart to heart?

With startling newness it became clear to me that *all* those "first priorities" which give richest meaning to life are dependent upon and determined by the place we give to *prayer*.

To others who may know "the barrenness of an overcrowded life" I recommend a similar deliberate self-confrontation. Do not say, "It is useless: I know the answers beforehand." You do not know them dynamically until they dominate you in such a way that you conform your whole life to them. Compel your mind slowly to weigh and answer. Then relate the answers to your own life, home, business, habits. Of this I am certain: you will give at least *one* answer which will align you with all the greatest saints who have ever lived. You will answer that *nothing* can be more important to your life and wellbeing than *REGULAR PRAYER*. You will believe this, not because others have said it, but because you have *seen* it.

Then, "strike while the iron is hot". Review your daily schedule. You will not now be doing so any more just to see where a hurried snatch of prayer can be furtively inserted. You will be so arranging things that all other commitments or usual activities of your free time must conform to the place you give to prayer. Prayer must be no longer a dot on the circumference, but the hub of the wheel; and you will soon find that all the wheel somehow runs more smoothly around that new hub. The "flesh" will still be as sluggish or resentful. The arch-enemy will tell his captains to discourage you. Unexpected time-encroachments may sneak up on you. But where godly resolve to pray is immersed in love to our Lord it always wins. What is more, with each victory of loving determination to put regular prayer *first,* the opposition grows weaker, communing becomes sweeter, and the presence of the risen Lord sheds its radiance through all the other hours of the day.

In the Bible there seem to be *four levels* of prayer indicated. It is (1) a necessity, (2) a duty, (3) a privilege, (4) a delight. On the first level, prayer is simply but sheerly a *necessity*. Without it godliness withers and the spiritual life atrophies. What air is to the lungs, or oxygen to bodily health, prayer is to our spiritual development. Even Bible knowledge becomes stale and lifeless apart from prayer, just as even a well-fed body ails and dies without fresh air. Observation convinces me that whatever uplifting visitations or sanctifying experiences may come to us at one time or another, none ever becomes continuous in our spiritual life apart from regular, unhurried, secret prayer-time. Prayerlessness is a spiritual grave.

But there is that higher level on which prayer is seen as a moral *duty*. As an expression of worship it is our duty to *God*. As a means of intercession it is our duty to *others*. As a means of sanctification it is a duty to *ourselves*. Because prayer is a duty, prayerlessness is sin. That is why Samuel said, "God forbid that I should *sin* against the Lord in ceasing to pray for you" (1 Sam.

12: 23). That aspect of prayerlessness as *sin* may well startle many of us.

Then there is that third level: prayer as a transcendent *privilege*. It gives access to the highest of all thrones, through the costliest of all sacrifices, with the readiest of all welcomes. There is no longer need to limp there in prodigals' rags; we are welcomed there as "sons of God" reinstated through the redeeming blood of Calvary. Our access never varies with our own fluctuating condition; it remains constant because it is on the basis of a finished atonement and an immutable covenant and an ever-efficacious Cross and an ever-prevailing Name. That such an all-eclipsing privilege can be treated indifferently by us must be an astonishment to angels!

But the highest level is when prayer becomes our dearest *delight*, opening up to us a heart-to-heart communion with God which is heaven begun below. So long as prayer is regarded as no higher than a necessity, a duty, or even as the loftiest of all privileges, it can never have its richest, loveliest meaning in our life. But when it has become a pure *delight*, a rapturous resort, a bliss of communion, a spontaneous heart-cry of holy desire, then we know not only the intercessory power of prayer but its exquisite inward reward.

When prayer becomes this dear delight of communion, its reflex influence upon the human mind is wonderfully healing and exhilarating. It releases the nervous system from tensions, relieves the mind from pressures, restores a true sense of values in life, and refreshes one's whole organism. It is then that we begin to hear, in our deepest consciousness, the soul-music of such promises as Isaiah 26: 3, "Thou wilt keep him in perfect peace whose mind is stayed on Thee"; and Psalm 91: 1, "He that dwelleth in the secret place of the Most High shall abide under the shadow of the Almighty"; and Philippians 4: 7, "The peace of God which passeth all understanding." The tired saint finds himself "mounting up with wings as eagles"; for in seasons of such praying there is a recreative therapy which does far more for the mind than all the diversions of the merely "natural man". I can bear witness from oft-proven experience that when my own prayer-life has been deepest, richest, most regular and lingering, my whole general health has been better. Life's burdens and daily toils remain, but the weight and drag are gone as we thus learn to lean continually on our heavenly Father's bosom. We sing with Charlotte Elliott—

My God, is any hour so sweet,
  From blush of morn to evening star,
As that which calls me to Thy feet,
  The hour of prayer?

Blest is that tranquil hour of morn,
  And blest that hour of solemn eve,
When on the wings of prayer upborne,
  The world I leave.

For then a dayspring shines on me,
  Brighter than morn's ethereal glow,
And richer dews descend from Thee
  Than earth can know.

Then is my strength by Thee renewed;
  Then are my sins by Thee forgiven;
Then dost Thou cheer my solitude
  With hope of heaven.

No words can tell what sweet relief
  There for my every want I find,
What strength for warfare, balm for grief,
  What peace of mind.

In my late 'teens, soon after my conversion to Christ, I read the *Autobiography* of John G. Paton, missionary to the New Hebrides. He was born in Scotland amid very humble circumstances, but he had a father who knew that high-level meaning of prayer. Let me quote: "Our home consisted of a 'but' and a 'ben',[1] and a mid-room or chamber called the 'closet'. . . . The closet was a very small apartment betwixt the other two, having room only for a bed, a little table, and a chair; with a diminutive window shedding a diminutive light on the scene. This was the *sanctuary* of that cottage home. Thither daily, and oftentimes a day, generally after each meal, we saw our father retire, and 'shut the door'; and we children got to understand by a sort of spiritual instinct (for the thing was too sacred to be talked about) that prayers were being poured out there for us, as of old by the High Priest within the veil in the Most Holy Place. We occasionally heard the echoes of a trembling voice, pleading as for life; and we learned to slip out and in past that door on tip-toe, not to disturb the holy colloquy. The outside world might not know, but we knew whence came that happy light as of a new-born smile which was always

[1] The kitchen and living room in the small, old-fashioned, two-room Scottish cottage.

dawning on my father's face: it was a reflection from the Divine Presence in the consciousness of which he lived. Never in temple or cathedral, in mountain or in glen, can I hope to feel that the Lord God is nearer or more visibly walking and talking with men, than under that humble cottage roof of thatch and oaken wattles."

A friend of mine in Canada used to tell me the same about *his* father. Each evening, after returning home from work, his father would wash and change, have his evening meal, then spend one hour alone in his bedroom, for prayer. Sometimes he would get home looking tired after an exacting day at his printing works; but again and again, after that hour alone with his Lord, he would emerge looking as refreshed as if he had been to some secret fountain of youth.

I have nothing to say against television *per se*; but who among the godly and morally decent can help deploring the large degree to which its usage is perverted? In my own judgment, so far as the larger amount of the programming goes, television is Satan's widest and deepest invasion of home life on this earth. Hundreds of thousands of Christian people who would never have darkened the doors of the modern cinema or theatre or dance hall now open their own doors to them all on the T.V. screen. Even the readings of the news, in America, must be interspersed with glamorized advertisements of beer and tobacco—which highway statistics and medical science now label as two of the worst killers. However, quite apart from that, the point I make here is, that what television may mean simply as a *diversion* to the natural man, *prayer* can mean, in a far higher way, to the spiritually minded man. Prayer, in its sublimest sense of communing with God, should be to the Christian a nerve-relaxing, tension-easing, mind-refreshing, spirit-elevating relief and release and renewal. That is precisely what Isaiah says about it: "They that wait upon the Lord shall *renew* their strength; they shall mount up with wings as eagles" (Isa. 40: 31).

That is the kind of prayer-life which makes divine guidance a *continuous* reality, as distinct from mere emergency guidance at critical intervals. It is a "walk with God", which brings the highest kind of guidance; for instead of guidance having to be given with outward signs before it can be discerned, there is inward communication from the heavenly Paraclete direct to the sensitively tuned-in believer.

Yea, closely art Thou with us, Lord!
  Neither in height nor depth to seek;
Thy guiding voice *within* is heard,
  Spirit to spirit Thou dost speak.

Do some whom I now address wonder whether such a prayer-life is possible? Such doubt evaporates as we listen to the many voices which bear witness to it! Blind Fanny Crosby, the gifted hymn-writer, knew something about it when she wrote,

Oh, the pure *delight* of a single hour
  Which before Thy throne I spend;
When I kneel in prayer and with Thee, my God,
  I commune as *friend with friend*!

During our twenty years sojourn in Edinburgh, Scotland, it was only natural that we should become the more familiar with oft-mentioned Scottish saints of two or three generations ago whose names are evergreens in the Scottish evangelical tradition. Think of that lovely character Horatius Bonar who passed to heavenly service less than seventy years ago. Oh, what a treasury of precious hymns his consecrated genius has left us! How some of us (especially in Britain) have thrilled and wept and communed with God in some of those hymns! Let me remind you of just a few by quoting their first verses.

"O love of God, how strong and true;
  Eternal, and yet ever new;
Uncomprehended and unbought,
  Beyond all knowledge and all thought."

"I bless the Christ of God.
  I rest on love divine;
And with unfaltering lip and heart
  I call this Saviour mine."

"I heard the voice of Jesus say,
  Come unto Me, and rest;
Lay down, thou weary one, lay down
  Thy head upon my breast!
I came to Jesus as I was,
  Weary, and worn, and sad;
I found in Him a resting-place,
  And He has made me glad."

"Go, labour on, spend and be spent,
    Thy joy to do the Father's will;
It is the way the Master went;
    Should not the servant tread it still?

"Fill Thou my life, O Lord my God,
    In every part with praise,
That my whole being may proclaim
    Thy being and Thy ways.
Not praising lips alone, I ask,
    Nor e'en a praising heart,
But all my life, O Lord, made up
    Of praise in every part."

Horatius Bonar's diary gives flashes of light on the wonderful communion with God which lay behind those hymns. In one place: "The Lord filled me with desire and made me feel that I must be as much with Him *alone* as with souls in public." In another place: "I must at once return, through the Lord's strength, to not less than three hours a day spent in prayer and meditation upon the Word." On the first day of his ministry at Finnieston, Glasgow: "Tomorrow I propose to spend most of the day in prayer in the church." And so we might go on quoting.

Perhaps Dr. Bonar's closest friend was Robert Murray McCheyne, whose prayerfulness was proverbial. Another of his friends was Dr. Moody Stuart whose testimony was: "I cannot say that a day passes without my beholding the beauty of the Lord, and being revived by His grace." There was William Hewitson of Dirleton, of whom Dr. Bonar says, "He seemed to have *no intervals* in his communion with God". Hewitson himself once remarked, "I am better acquainted with Jesus than with any friend I have on earth."

I shall be reminded that all these men of God were *ministers,* and that they therefore had much more time for prayer than most other people. From my own experience, however, I rather doubt whether ministers *do* have the more time. Most men have a fixed starting and stopping time for their daily work, outside of which their time is their own; not so the usual minister; he is on call all hours of the day. But be that as it may, is it not true with most of us that we have *far* more available time for prayer than we devote to it? Maybe we cannot give three consecutive hours a day, like Luther and Wesley and others, nor is that a necessity to the kind of rich fellowship with God about which we are speaking.

With most of us the simple first need is *desire plus resolution*. To our last day on earth the desire for prayer will *always* need to be reinforced by resolution; though the testimony of the Lord's overcomers is, that where resolution persists it gradually grows stronger and easier, until prayer becomes the most natural and continuous occupation of the heart.

Even when, through regular waitings upon God, we know something of the Spirit-filled life and the manifesting of Jesus to the heart (John 14: 21) we shall still need that firm resolve; for the "flesh" will still be indisposed; and the invisible foe will never run bankrupt of diversionary stratagems; and new things to do will elbow out our set times for prayer if we are unwary. Mark well: it is even about praying "in the Spirit" that Paul says, in Ephesians 6: 18, "Praying always with all prayer and supplication in the Spirit, and watching thereunto *with all perseverance* and supplication for all saints". Ferrar Fenton's translation is, "keeping watch in it with *steady tenacity*"! Yes, that is the golden key which unlocks the gates to all the bigger blessings of the prayer-life:

"KEEPING WATCH IN IT WITH STEADY TENACITY"

Dr. Moody Stuart, already mentioned, had a threefold rule: (a) Pray till you pray; (b) Pray till you are conscious of being heard; (c) Pray till you receive an answer. I think we all know what he meant by "Pray till you *pray*". As in the old Hebrew tabernacle, so is it in the prayer life: there is the "outer court"; then the inner "holy place"; then the inmost "holy of holies". We need to pray right through the first two, to the holy of holies; till all voices of the outer court and even the intrusive voices of our own self-wisdom are hushed, and we are "beyond the veil", consciously alone with God.

Another aspect of habitual prayer which many of us need deliberately to re-think and re-assess is its *practical* value. Is there not a subtle idea deceiving many of us, that too much prayer is *un*practical? Once for all that misapprehension needs to be faced and repudiated. The exemplary men and women of prayer have always been the most effective *doers*, from Paul to Luther, from Luther to Wesley, from Wesley to Charles G. Finney and D. L. Moody, and C. H. Spurgeon, and William Booth of the Salvation Army. The famous Puritan, Thomas Hooker, wrote, "Prayer is my chief work, and it is by means of it that I carry on all the rest." It is just as true today that those who pray well always work best and accomplish most. Indeed they achieve most with least waste of time and energy because they are divinely directed. So long as we secrete the supposition that protracted prayer is unpractical it will paralyse resolution.

Still another point which needs oft-mention is that there cannot be *continuity* of heavenly communion or guidance apart from regular *set seasons* of prayer. We sometimes hear it said: "Prayer does not consist merely in stated times of withdrawment; it is meant to go on all day between the soul and God, even amid our busiest occupations." That is true, but it becomes misleading if we divorce it from the proven *other* truth that such all-through-the-day communion *dies* apart from set times of withdrawment for prayer. By parallel it might be said, "Physical health does not consist merely in three stated meals a day: it is meant to go on all day, through exercise and fresh air." But leave out those set meals, and see how long you remain healthy—or even alive! The importance of regular prayer-times is emphasized all through the Bible either in stated instruction or by moving example.

Our Lord Jesus Himself is both the highest teacher and the truest example of such recurrent appointments with God. There is a notable comment in Luke 5: 16, "He withdrew himself into the wilderness, and prayed." In the Greek, "wilderness" is plural, meaning lonely *places*; and the word "withdrew" is a present participle, meaning *continual* withdrawings. Also, the word "prayed" is another present participle, indicating prayings *going on*. A close translation would be, "He was retiring into the deserts and praying." It was not just one withdrawal, not just one secluded spot, not just one prayer, but many. *The Twentieth Century New Testament* gives the sense:

"JESUS USED TO WITHDRAW TO LONELY PLACES AND PRAY"

Significantly enough, Luke makes this comment at one of the busiest parts of our Lord's ministry. The hours were filled with huge crowds to be taught, many invalids to be healed, hard questions to be answered, instructions to be given. There was scarce leisure to eat. But amid it all, *"Jesus used to withdraw to lonely places and pray"*. Moreover, besides rich communion, much of His praying must have been interceding, pleading, seek-

ing strength and guidance. Presumably, some of His prayers at
that time were part of those referred to in Hebrews 5: 7, "Who in
the days of His flesh offered up prayers and supplications with
strong crying and tears." Dr. M. M'Intyre well observes, "And
this One who sought retirement with so much solicitude was the
Son of God, having no sin to confess, no shortcoming to deplore,
no unbelief to subdue, no languor of love to overcome. . . . If it
was part of the sacred discipline of the incarnate Son of God that
He should observe frequent seasons of retirement, how much
more is it incumbent on *us*, broken as we are and disabled by
manifold sin, to be diligent in the exercise of private prayer?"

Many of us need to bring this to a practical issue in our life. It
has been truly said that for most of us the threefold problem is
that of getting (1) a quiet *place*, (2) a quiet *time*, (3) a quiet *mind*.

As to the first—a quiet place, *determine to find one*, and you
will. Have you ever thought how awkward it must have been for
our Lord to find aloneness in that Nazareth home? Let me quote
Dr. M. M'Intyre again:

> "In the carpenter's cottage in Nazareth there were, it
> appears, no fewer than nine persons who lived under the one
> roof. There were Jesus, and Mary his mother, and Joseph.
> There were also the Lord's 'brothers'—four of them—
> and at least two 'sisters'. The cottage consisted principally
> of a living room, a workshop, and an inner chamber, or a
> store-closet, in which the provision for the day, the kitchen
> utensils, the firewood, etc., were laid. That gloomy recess
> had a latch on the inner side, placed there, it may be, by the
> carpenter's Son; for that dark chamber was His sanctum, not
> less sacred than the cloud-wrapt shrine of the Presence in the
> Temple."

Later, when our Lord had left Nazareth, often having "not
where to lay His head", He made the bare solitudes His prayer-
room. Or, when in the city, He would find some nearby garden,
such as Gethsemane, and there, amid the trees, beneath the stars,
He would out-pray the night.

> "Cold mountains and the midnight air
>   Witnessed the fervour of Thy prayer;
> The deserts Thy communings knew,
>   Thy conflicts and Thy victory too."

During the Second World War, Sir Winston Churchill used to carry a black silk handkerchief, and when, through deprivation of night-time sleep, he would become drowsy during the day, he would draw this handkerchief over his head, cover his eyes, and slip off into a relieving doze. Similarly, there was a hard-pressed Christian wife and mother in the poorer part of a large city who seemed scarcely ever free from the insistent clamour of household demands, yet she maintained such glad communion with Christ that someone asked her secret. She replied, "I throw my apron over my head, and right there is my prayer-room." Few of us are as hard put to as that, to find a place for our regular prayer-tryst; but whatever the deterrents, love and determination will find *somewhere* sanctifiable.

Perhaps, for some, the more disconcerting problem is to fix on a regularly available *time*. Let us face up to it: for most of us there will be a price to pay (let us be grateful to pay it!). At some point there will be need for self-denial; maybe our having to let go some weekly pleasure hour, or some nightly diversion, or some careless disuse of time. If we decide to make the *first* hour of each day our special prayer-time, it may mean going to bed an hour earlier at night, and getting up an hour earlier at morn. John Wesley is a stimulating example of watching the clock at night for the sake of that hour the next morning. Undoubtedly there are reasons why the first hour of the day has unique advantages; but it may *not* be a workable time in some circumstances. Each must decide according to individual necessities. If it *can* be early morn, it should be complemented by briefer follow-ups at noon and evening. If it cannot be till evening there should be briefer anticipations at early morn and noon. The vital thing is to fix the time or times and build the *habit*.

Finally, we need the quiet *mind*. This, to some of us, may seem the biggest difficulty of all. Oh, these non-stop minds! This upstart imagination! This memory which persistently digs things up from the subconscious at the wrong times! This seemingly incurable thought-wandering during prayer! How do we *acquire* the "quiet mind"? Well, this is another place where the experience of others can encourage us. Their testimony is, that the quiet mind develops with the prayer *habit*. Will it seem too kindergarten if I offer a few simple suggestions to those who wonder how they can fill a whole hour with prayer? or how they can cure mind-wandering?

First: this is a good usual order: (1) express worship and adoration to God; (2) then express thanksgiving for all your many blessings: see Philippians 4: 6, (3) intercede for others, whose names you have on a written list, (4) then pray for yourself, your deepest needs and longings. This order saves our prayer-times from deadly egocentricity and from interminable mere "asking".

Second: preface your praying by briefly meditating on a passage of Scripture. For this it is good to be going through the Gospels or some Epistle—a paragraph or so a day.

Third: pray steadily through an Epistle; so many verses each day; turning every exhortation, every challenge, every promise, every warning, into a prayer for its operation in your own life. This can make your prayer-hour so rich, it will be much too short! You will begrudge every merciless tick of the clock!

Fourth: use your hymn book. Make a list of all the best prayer-hymns, and *pray* them. Some of them will so surprise you and draw you out in longing prayer that you will keep coming back to re-pray them. Pray till your spiritual experience is up to the level of our best hymns.

To the foregoing simple recommendations I would add just two or three more. First, let intercession for *others* claim a large part of your praying. Paul did (Rom. 1: 9, Eph. 1: 16, Phil. 1: 4, Col. 1: 9, 1 Thess. 1: 2). Many of us would find new liberation from captivity to trial, doubt, problems, if we prayed more for others and less for ourselves. Remember Job 42: 10. "And the Lord turned the captivity of Job when he prayed for *his friends*" —not for himself!

Do not over-complicate your prayer-life with too many subject-divisions. You are coming to a FATHER, not an accountant. Yet on the other hand *do* have some simple but sufficient system. In my own missionary praying I have found it useful to have a map of the world sectioned into a weekly cycle. Use *written* memos and names. A Chinese proverb says, "the strongest memory is weaker than the weakest ink."

Always have one part of your prayer-period for *silent listening*. It is good that much of our praying should be in either outwardly or inwardly spoken words; but there is a language of the soul too deep for actual words. There is also a *silence* before God which speaks even *more* deeply—and at the same time *hears* God as only silence can. Remember young Samuel's words, "Speak, Lord, for Thy servant *heareth*" (1 Sam. 3: 9, 10). Some of us tend continually to transpose it: "Hear, Lord, for Thy servant speaketh." Practise *listening*! Never forget that last, seven-fold call of the Bible: "He that hath ears to *hear*, let him hear what the *Spirit* saith to the Churches" (Rev. 2, 3). God needs listeners as well as pleaders.

What a subject is this matter of prayer! What books have been written on it through the centuries! What meaning it has had in the redeeming purpose of God and the sanctifying of the saints! Were it not for the inherent value and urgency of the subject we would be apologising for such inadequate reference to it here. But what we *have* said in these pages has been simply to underline its importance in the Christian life, and its indispensable place if we would know what Samuel Shoemaker calls "the *upper level* of guidance."

Living on that upper level of divine guidance is the only thing, says Dr. Shoemaker, which will bring back to us today "the lost *radiance* of the Christian religion"—that radiance which is the "outer shining of the inner light". That sunlit "upper level" is inviting you and me today; and it is well worth the climb! To the heart which has become habitually prayerful, guidance is no longer a mootable hypothesis, it is a glad *certitude*. That which above all else makes guidance real and constant is a reverent familiarity with the *Guide*.

THOSE STRANGE DELAYS

Strive to see God in all things without exception, and acquiesce in His will with absolute submission. Do everything for God, uniting yourself to Him by a mere upward glance, or by the overflowing of your heart towards Him. Never be in a hurry; do everything quietly and in a calm spirit. Do not lose your inward peace for anything whatsoever, even if your whole world seems upset. Commend all to God, and then lie still and be at rest in His bosom. Whatever happens, abide steadfast in a determination to cling simply to God, trusting in His eternal love for you; and if you find that you have wandered forth from His shelter, recall your heart quietly and simply. Maintain a holy simplicity of mind, and do not smother yourself with a host of cares, wishes, or longings, under any pretext.

*From the writings of a
16th century Saint.*

10

THOSE STRANGE DELAYS

ANY realistic study of divine guidance in human lives must take into account the problem posed by divine *delays*. In asking God for His guidance or for His gracious answer to some other urgent request, how many of us, at one time or another, have mistaken delay for denial! We need to watch against that easy fault, for the discouragement which it engenders often results in our discontinuance of asking, or else provokes us impatiently to presume that Heaven's silence gives us reason to act on our own, without any further waiting. It seems wise, therefore, that we should consider carefully this matter of divine delays (whether real or merely seeming), and see if we may get light on it from Scripture.

My mind goes back to a sermon which I preached on this theme, years ago, in Edinburgh, Scotland. Its title was: *The Delays of Jesus*, and its introductory text was John 6: 17, "It was now dark, and Jesus was not come to them." That sermon was preached just as the Second World War was ending with the collapse of Nazi Germany and the suicide of Adolf Hitler. Sitting in our church on a Sunday morning was a padre who at that time was over in Britain with the American forces. Now that the war was over, at least in its European theatre, his heart had been thrilling at the thought of his soon being returned to America, to his precious wife, and to his dear little son whom he had not yet even seen, owing to prolonged war-time absence. Then, like a sudden, stunning blow, word had come that he was assigned to immediate new duty in Japan for an indefinite period. His despondency as he sat in our Sunday morning service, with that on his mind, need not be described. Earnest prayer, mounting hope, and now this sudden, sickening *delay*! I did not know him, had never met him, and knew nothing of his sadness, but I had at least one unusually attentive hearer that morning when I announced as my subject: the problem of divinely permitted *delays*!

And now, just recently, I have been privileged to hold meetings at a large church in Texas. Its beloved pastor is one of the most gifted, consecrated ministers whom I have ever had the pleasure to serve. I did not know him until then, and was surprised when he told me that he had met me and heard me preach twenty years earlier. He took from a locked drawer his carefully treasured war diary, and read to me his record of that Sunday morning service in Edinburgh, Scotland, twenty years earlier, and how God had spoken to him through that discourse on divine delays!

That sermon has never been printed, taped, or even preached again from then until now; but I have a feeling that it should have a resurrection in these pages. Whether it seems the propitious thing to reintroduce it here, practically as it was given then, I will not stay to determine; but it seems to speak the very word which I am wanting to say here on this problem of divine delays. So, here it is.

THE DELAYS OF JESUS

"It was now dark, and Jesus was not come to them"
—John 6: 17.

These words take our thoughts back to a dark and stormy night on the Sea of Galilee long ago. A small vessel lurched and lunged and creaked and groaned amid the swirling waves of a heavy storm. A point had come when oars seemed useless, and hope was almost gone. One thought alone—one anxious, puzzled, almost despairing thought—betrayed itself through the strained looks of those twelve men on board: Why had the Master not come? Had they not rightly understood Him to mean that He would be with them long ere this? Yet "it was now dark and Jesus was not come to them". Why, why the delay?

Such is the immediate connection of the text. But look at the words again: "It was now dark, and Jesus was not come to them." Do the words suggest anything beyond their immediate connection? I think they do. They somehow open a theme which, although it may seem strange at first, is of very tender concern to all Christian hearts. I mean *the delays of Jesus*.

All of us who have had any mentionable experience of the Christian life have had times when we, too, have been perplexed by the delays, or seeming delays, of our heavenly Master. He has sometimes kept us waiting (though with a gracious purpose which we did not know at the time) until we were at the point of soul-agony, and we groaned, like those long-ago disciples, "It is now *dark,* and Jesus has not come."

In the Gospel records there are *three* noteworthy instances of such delay by our Lord Jesus, and we may learn much from them for our guidance and comfort. Let me call your attention to them again, just here. First, there is the delay with which our text is connected, namely, our Lord's delay in going to the disciples on the night of that severe storm. Second, there was His seemingly unsympathetic delay while on the way to heal the daughter of Jairus. Third, there was His strange delay before going to Bethany after receiving word from Martha and Mary, "Lord, behold, he whom Thou lovest is sick."

Yes, I think we may learn much from these delays of Jesus; and it will help us if we consider them in a threefold way: (1) their outward strangeness, (2) their inward purpose, (3) their lasting message.

Their Outward Strangeness

So, then, to begin with, we notice *their outward strangeness.* How strange indeed seemed our Lord's delay in relieving those disciples amid that pounding night-storm on Galilee! The incident is recorded by Matthew and Mark and John. They make quite clear that the storm was a bad one; but the most striking evidence of its fury and the plight of the disciples is supplied by John's remark that when at last Jesus walked to them over the turmoiled waters, they had rowed only "five and twenty or thirty furlongs" (three miles or so) even though it was now "the fourth watch of the night" (Matt. 14: 25). Formerly the Jews had divided the night into three watches, but after Palestine became a Roman province the Roman division into four was adopted. The first watch ran from 6 p.m. till 9; the second from 9 till midnight; the third from 12 o'clock midnight till 3 a.m., and the "fourth watch of the night" was from 3 a.m. till 6 a.m., at which point daytime reckoning began again. So, then, if our Lord came to them in "the fourth watch", they had been struggling with the oars from evening onward (John 6: 16) for over nine or ten hours—and, after all that, they had covered only three miles or so! To all appearances they were in acute peril, yet Jesus made no move to go to them until that darkest hour just before the dawn; and His delay is made all the stranger by Mark's comment that from the mountain elevation where our Lord prayed "He *saw them toiling* in rowing".

But now we leave that storm for a very different scene. In Mark 5: 22–36 we see our Lord's delay *while on His way to heal the daughter of Jairus*. The account reads:

"And, behold, there cometh one of the rulers of the synagogue, Jairus by name; and when he saw Jesus, he fell at His feet, and besought Him greatly, saying, My little daughter lieth at the point of death: I pray thee, come and lay thy hands on her, that she may be healed; and she shall live. And Jesus went with him; and much people followed him, and thronged him. And a certain woman, which had an issue of blood twelve years, and had suffered many things of many physicians, and had spent all that she had, and was nothing bettered, but rather grew worse, when she had heard of Jesus, came in the press behind, and touched his garment. For she said, If I may touch but his clothes, I shall be whole. And straightway the fountain of her blood was dried up; and she felt in her body that she was healed of that plague. And Jesus, immediately knowing in himself that virtue had gone out of him, turned him about in the press, and said, Who touched my clothes? His disciples said unto him, Thou seest the multitude thronging thee, and sayest thou, Who touched me? And he looked round about to see her that had done this thing. But the woman fearing and trembling, knowing what was done in her, came and fell down before him, and told him all the truth. And he said unto her, Daughter, thy faith hath made thee whole; go in peace, and be whole of thy plague. While he yet spake, there came from the ruler of the synagogue's house certain which said, Thy daughter is dead: why troublest thou the Master any further? As soon as Jesus heard the word that was spoken, he saith unto the ruler of the synagogue, Be not afraid, only believe."

Our Lord's unhurrying delay here, to single out and speak to that anonymous woman who had touched the fringe of His robe, would seem exasperatingly needless and unsympathetic to the overwrought father of the dying girl. Synagogue-ruler Jairus must have been agonized by the fear that while our Lord lingered the life of his dying child was fast ebbing away. Our Lord not only took time to hear some of the thronging people deny having touched Him, and time to wait for the woman to confess, but with no sense of hurry He tarried to pronounce a blessing upon her in the hearing of the crowd. The anxious father's fear, alas, was confirmed. While Jesus still lingered, speaking to the woman, messengers came from the house of the synagogue ruler to say that any further appeal to Jesus was of no use; the little maid had died. To that broken-hearted father the delay must have been tantalizing. Had he not told Jesus that it was a matter of only minutes if his child was to be snatched from death? Jesus *could* have got there, just in the nick of time, if only He had not aggravatingly lingered with the crowd and that woman! Yes, the delay did seem strange.

But now we turn to what is perhaps the strangest delay of all, that is, our Lord's delay *before going to Bethany after learning that Lazarus was ill.* The Lazarus episode is related in the eleventh chapter of John, and is so well known that we scarcely need quote at length from it. But note carefully again what is said about the delay in verses 5, 6 and 7.

"Now Jesus loved Martha, and her sister, and Lazarus. When He had heard therefore that Lazarus was sick, He abode two days still in the same place where He was. Then after that He saith to His disciples, Let us go into Judæa again."

There is a strange-seeming deliberateness about our Lord's delay here which marks it off from the other two delays. His delay in going to the storm-tossed disciples might be put down in some degree to His preoccupation in prayer; and His delay on the way to heal Jairus's daughter might be extenuatingly excused on the ground that He halted to confer healing on another sufferer who had just as much claim upon Him as the little girl. But here, in connection with Lazarus, the delay is *deliberate.*

Notice that strange "therefore" in verse 6. "Now Jesus *loved* Martha and her sister and Lazarus . . . *therefore* when He had heard that Lazarus was sick He abode two days . . . where He was." It seemed a contradictory way of showing love![1] Plainly,

[1] Moffatt's translation transplants the fifth verse and puts it between verses 2 and 3 so as to reduce the awkwardness of the "therefore" in verse 6; but so far as I can find, there is no variation in the Greek manuscript to warrant Moffatt's taking such a liberty with the text.

Lazarus's illness was considered dangerous. Otherwise the sisters would not have sent for our Lord to come; for Bethany was near Jerusalem, where quite recently the Jews had tried to stone Jesus, as the sisters well knew. Evidently Martha and Mary were anxious. Yet although our Lord had such special love for them and for Lazarus, He deliberately delayed for those two days! And, as we gather from verses 7 and 11, it was just at the end of those two days that Lazarus died! Bethabara beyond Jordan was about two days distance by foot to Bethany; so our Lord *could* have got there before illness gave place to death. Moreover, even *after* those two days, He evidently lingered on the journey, for when He reached Bethany Lazarus had already been four days in the tomb (the entombing presumably having taken place on the day of demise, according to Palestinian custom). Certainly, the delay would seem strange to Martha and Mary—very strange indeed.

Their Inward Purpose

Well, such was the outward strangeness of those three delays. Let us now look at them a little more closely, to see their *inward purpose*.

The first thing which becomes obvious is that those delays simply had to be as they were, in order *to demonstrate our Lord's supreme power* in a never-to-be-forgotten way. In the first incident there had to be delay till the storm had lasted long enough for those storm-battered boatmen to become beaten and baffled by it. Only so would they realize in the intended way our Lord's uttermost power over Nature. (See Matt. 14: 33, Mark 6: 52).

In the second incident there had to be delay long enough for the dread news to come to Jairus that the worst had happened; that the little one was actually dead. Only so could our Lord demonstrate His power, not only over disease, but even over death.

In the third incident our Lord must delay long enough for the body of Lazarus to have started decomposing. Only thus could our Lord make it clear that at the resurrection of Lazarus his very soul was being recalled from Sheol or Hades to reinhabit the restored body.

Thus, through those three delays, our Lord Jesus was able to demonstrate with classic finality His power over *Nature* and over *Death* and over *Hades*.

But besides this, a further purpose of those delays was *to develop the faith of the disciples*. In connection with the first delay, hear our Lord's words to Peter, "O thou of *little faith,* wherefore didst thou *doubt?*" In connection with the second delay, hear His words to Jairus, "Be not afraid; only *believe.*" In connection with the third delay, hear His words to Martha, "Said I not unto thee that if thou wouldst *believe* thou shouldst see the glory of God?"

After that first delay, would those disciples ever forget the ghost-like Figure treading down the very waves? After that second delay, would Jairus ever forget our Lord's words, *"Talitha cumi"?* After that third delay, would the spectators ever forget the death-conquering shout of Jesus into the mouth of the dark tomb, "Lazarus, come forth"?

There may have been other purposes, too, in those three delays, but all I stay to point out here is, that in each case there was new exhibition of our Lord's sovereign power; and a new lesson on faith; a new revelation of the divine, and a new education of the human; a new demonstration that often the disciples' direst extremity is the Master's truest opportunity. This brings me to my final observation concerning those three delays of Jesus, namely:

Their Lasting Message

The first big object-lesson in them is that *our Lord can transform the most hopeless circumstances.* See the extreme plight of those disciples in that storm. They had rowed three hours, from 6 p.m. until 9, and seen daylight turn to stormy dusk. They had toiled another three hours, 9 o'clock till 12 midnight, and seen stormy dusk become tempestuous night. They had struggled yet another three hours in blackness and howling storm. Strength was exhausted; the storm was unabating; oars were now useless; and where were they? The Sea of Galilee is roughly twelve miles north to south and about six east to west; so if they had gone about three miles they were now right in the middle, at the spasm-centre of the storm, in thick darkness, with their strength petered out. Could the circumstances have seemed more hopeless?

Similarly, when the pallid-faced young daughter of Jairus had become a motionless corpse on her couch, could the situation have seemed more hopeless? When dead brother Lazarus had lain enwrapped by rigid embalmings four days in a sepulchre, could the situation have seemed more hopeless? Yet in each case it was at hopeless zero-point that our Lord, the Master of surprises, suddenly turned disaster into deliverance, tragedy into triumph, sighing into singing, and deepest mystery into highest meaning.

Christian believer, take this precious fact to heart; keep it gratefully in mind; it can steady you and comfort you amid many "an horror of great darkness" (Gen. 15: 12). No situation is "too far gone" for our all-controlling Lord to overrule and transform. I have experienced this at unforgettable crises in my own life. When the very "sentence of death" has been written (as it would seem) at the very point of "no hope" the Lord has silently but surely brought light out of darkness, joy out of sorrow, pearls out of tears, even as Samson's bees brought honey out of the lion's carcass. Do I address someone even now who is in deep problem, almost to the point of despair? Take heart! Though things seem to have gone beyond "redemption-point", though you seem to be in the swift current just above the falls, though you cannot figure out how even God could alter things for you now except by ending the world's history, He knows better than you. He is the Master-Planner of eleventh-hour deliverances. Let both Scripture and the voice of Christian experience convince you that again and again the blackest sky has been suddenly enringed by the brightest rainbow; the weeping willow has become the victory-palm; and the "dews of sorrow" have suddenly become lustrous with precious evidences of Heaven's loving-kindness!

> I know not by what methods rare,
> But this I know, God answers prayer:
> I know that He has given His word,
> Which pledges prayer is always heard,
> And will be answered, soon or late ;
> So let me pray and calmly wait.
>
> I know not if the blessing sought
> Will come in just the way I thought ;
> I leave my prayer with Him alone
> Whose will is wiser than my own ;
> Assured that He will grant my quest,
> Or send an answer far more blest.

But, now, another reassuring lesson which we learn from those delays of Jesus is, that *our greatest discoveries and blessings often come through our sorest trials.* When our Lord walked across the waves to that rocking boat, not only did the storm thereupon subside into gentle calm, but, as John 6: 21 says, "Immediately the ship was at the land whither they went". Our Lord's delayed answers are always the quickest way to blessing. In the case of Jairus, not only did he meet Jesus the healer, but suddenly he discovered himself face to face with "God who raiseth the dead" (2 Cor. 1: 9). As for the raising of Lazarus, the biggest discovery and joy of their life came thereby to Martha and Mary. They had already entertained the dearest thoughts of Jesus; but now, at one and the same time, they saw the most touching evidence of His humanness as He "wept" at their brother's grave, and the most overpowering evidence of His deity as He proved Himself "the Resurrection and the Life"!

Tired and troubled Christian, beware of thinking that God is harsh as you drag along amid permitted sorrow or tribulation. It is easy, when the mind is tortured by suffering or tensed by pain, to attribute fantastic ugliness to God. How His great father-heart must be grieved by this! If only we could grasp this fact: it is His permitting and overruling of calamities which leads to our most exalting and refining discoveries! Let Robert W. Service's lines bear witness to that fact:

> I sought Him on the purple seas;
>   I sought Him on the peaks aflame;
> Amid the gloom of giant trees
>   And canyons lone, I called His name.
> The wasted ways of earth I trod;
> In vain! In vain! I found not God.
>
> I sought Him in the lives of men,
>   In cities grand, in hamlets grey,
> In temples old beyond our ken,
>   And tabernacles of today.
> All life I sought from cloud to clod.
> In vain! In vain! I found not God.
>
> Then, after roaming far and wide,
>   In streets and seas and deserts wild,
> I came at last to stand beside
>   The death-bed of my little child.
> Lo, as I bent beneath the rod,
> I raised my eyes . . . and *there* was *GOD*!

A final lesson which comes to us is, that *in divine delays there is always a gracious purpose*. Our Lord could do no other than wait until those storm-tossed disciples had come to an end of self-struggling. Equally so, He had to let the little girl die if His bigger purpose was to be fulfilled. Again, it was altogether necessary that Lazarus should be dead and buried a full four days so that a competent number of witnesses might have time to gather; also in order that both the death and the resurrection-miracle might be indisputable facts even to hostile observers. The delay, with its seeming lack of tenderness toward the mourning sisters, was needful because wider interests than those of a single family were involved. In each of those long-ago delays of Jesus there was a rich and gracious purpose.

Dear fellow-believer, try to learn this truth deeply: there is always gracious purpose in divine delays toward *you*. Try to remember this: delay does not mean that God is neglecting you, much less that He has forsaken you. Be persuaded of this, also, that delayed answer to your prayer does not mean *denial* of your prayer. How readily many of us jump to the drastic conclusion that God has said, "No," when in truth He has said nothing! Do I need to remind you that there is a big difference between saying, "No," and saying nothing? A young fellow asks his father for a sum of money which, so he says, he urgently needs. If the father plainly says, "No," that settles it; but if he says nothing the son waits hopefully. If a young man asks a young woman to marry him, and she replies a definite "No", that settles it; but if she says nothing his heart still flutters with hope.

We should try to realize that if God's highest purposes for us are to be effected, delays in granting our prayers are often necessary. Sometimes, in our own hearts, there are unsuspected hindrances which need to be removed before there can be a safe "Yes" to us. As I myself now look back over some of the prayers I have prayed, how glad I am that God did not say "Yes"! (Do not others of you feel the same?). It was not always that God said a direct "No" to me, but there first had to be inward tutoring, discipline, sanctification, guidance, to make the "yes" safe— and that meant time, process, *delay*. A box of matches is very useful to mother in the kitchen; but don't give it to that rascally young child unless you want the house on fire! That sharp knife is very useful to daddy; but don't give it to that little boy who is crying for it, unless you want him to hurt himself! Try to remember, dear Christian, *God* has a plan for you, as well as your own! His is always safe and best for you: *yours* may be otherwise! The thing which you want most *could* be the most dangerous!

There is one other thing I would add. Sometimes God may say, "Yes"; sometimes He may say "No"; sometimes, instead of either "Yes" or "No", He may answer by *delay*—a delay with a bigger blessing in view than either an immediate "Yes" or an immediate "No" could confer. But this is certain: *no* sincere prayer in the Name of Jesus is ever left *unanswered*; and delay is always with a view to an answer bigger and better than that for which we asked.

> Ungranted yet, the prayer your lips have pleaded
>   In agony of heart these many years?
> Does faith begin to fail, is hope departing?
>   And think you all in vain your falling tears?
> Say not the Father has not heard your prayer;
> Full answer there shall be, sometime, somewhere.
>
> Ungranted yet? though when you first presented
>   This one petition at the Father's throne,
> It seemed you could not wait the time of asking
>   So urgent was your heart to make it known:
> Though years have passed, pray on, do not despair,
> Such prayer must answered be, sometime, somewhere.
>
> Ungranted yet? Nay, do not say "unanswered";
>   Perhaps *your* part is not yet wholly done;
> The work began when first your prayer was uttered
>   And God will finish what He has begun.
> If you still keep the incense burning there,
> His answer you *shall* see, sometime, somewhere!
>
> Ungranted yet? Faith cannot be unanswered;
>   Her feet are firmly planted on the *Rock*;
> Amid the wildest storm she stands undaunted,
>   Nor quails amid the loudest thunder shock.
> She moves Omnipotence to hear her prayer
> And cries it shall be done, sometime, somewhere!

A certain godly couple had three boys, and brought them up in the Christian faith. They not only prayed *for* them, they prayed *with* them, teaching them the *habit* of prayer. Yet as those three lads grew up into healthy youths they did not share or profess any such godliness as that of their parents. Then their mother died, but the father kept on praying for them and with them. He always gathered them round him for family prayers at an old, cane-seated chair; and oh, what prayers he prayed for them, kneeling at that old, cane-seated chair! Eventually the father himself died—when the three sons were grown men, all very successful in business, but never having made any Christian profession. After the funeral the three sons came back to settle what should be done about the furniture and other matters. One of them suggested, "Let's give these things to the elderly woman who has been looking after father." The eldest brother replied, "Well, I'm quite agreeable, except for this: I would like to have that old, cane-bottomed chair. I never heard prayers like those which dear dad prayed for us at that chair." As he spoke his voice trembled, and tears were in his eyes. Neither could the other two brothers conceal their emotion. Then the eldest brother said, "Let's kneel down again at that old, cane-bottomed chair." They did so; and one said to another, "If I had to live my life over again, I would not live without prayer and without God." Tears flowed; and there, at that old, cane-seated chair, all three brothers gave themselves to Christ. Two of them left business and went abroad as Christian missionaries, and the other brother, also, became a fervent public servant of the Lord. Neither the mother nor the father lived on earth to see the answer to their prayers; but the answer came—and somehow I think they knew up in heaven.

Dear Christian, buffeted by the billows, or praying with tears over smarting problems, and downcast by this puzzle of divine delay, be comforted. The God who bled to save you on Calvary loves you too well ever to mock you! Can you be more dismayed than the poet William Cowper must have been by his recurrent mental affliction? Yet it was he who glimpsed the sun-shaft through the draping gloom, and wrote,

> Ye fearful saints, fresh courage take!
>   The clouds ye so much dread
> Are big with mercy, and shall break
>   In blessings on your head!
>
> Blind unbelief is sure to err,
>   And scan God's work in vain;
> God is His own interpreter,
>   And He will make it plain.

Matthew and Mark and John all tell us that when our Lord walked the waves and drew near to the scared disciples, His first word which rang out to them across the waters was, *"Be of good cheer! It is I; be not afraid!"* He comes to *you*, this very day, across the troubled waters of your wondering and questioning. He calls to you now, not just from the New Testament page, but in your innermost consciousness,

"BE OF GOOD CHEER! IT IS I; BE NOT AFRAID!"

WALKING IN THE LIGHT

The "pure in heart" may not have much share in this world's honours and prosperity. These things fall for the most part into the hands of those who are guided by the maxims of selfish prudence. The single heart is often constrained by its love of the good to choose a path which it knows quite well leads away from the prizes coveted by men of the world. Such a choice the world laughs at. Singleness of mind in such cases appears to men of commonplace morality, foolishness bordering on imbecility. And from their point of view they judge rightly. Nevertheless waste not your pity on this "fool", as you call him. He obtains that which he values more than all he misses. He loses the world, but by way of compensation he attains to the vision of God. He beholds God's face in righteousness, and is satisfied when he awakes with His likeness.

A. B. Bruce.

11

WALKING IN THE LIGHT

As WE come to this last link in our chain of reflections on divine guidance, I cannot think of anything more appropriate than our listening again to the "voice from heaven" as it speaks to us through I John I: 7, *"If we walk in the light, as He is in the light, we have fellowship one with another, and the blood of Jesus Christ His Son cleanseth us from all sin."*

In this oft-quoted text a big door swings on a small hinge. The big, inviting door is the divine promise of "fellowship" and "cleansing". The little hinge on which that dual promise swings is the significant monosyllabic, "if"—"if we walk in the light as He is in the light".

The "fellowship" here promised is usually and rightly understood in an horizontal sense as between Christian and Christian—"fellowship one with another"; but I believe it also has a perpendicular upreach meaning fellowship with God Himself. Indeed, some Greek manuscripts actually read "fellowship with *Him*". Of course, all fellowship between Christian and Christian has its ground and sphere in our individual fellowship with God Himself. This the context noticeably emphasises: "That which we have seen and heard declare we unto you that ye also may have fellowship with us; and truly our fellowship is with *the Father* and with His Son, Jesus Christ" (3).

The "cleansing" here promised is a continuous cleansing from both the outward guilt and the inward stain of sin; that is, from the guilt of it before God, and the stain of it in our own conscience. The ever-abiding efficacy of the once-for-all propitiation keeps us clean in God's sight, so that there need be no interrupting of our fellowship with Him.

But, as we have said, everything depends on that "if". Look carefully at it again: "If we walk in the light. . . . ." It is only when we are walking in the light that the promise swings wide open. When you and I really "walk in the light, as He is in the light", then, and only then, we become distinctly *conscious* of our continual cleansing through the precious blood, and of our open access to the Father, and of His delight in us, and of an unobstructed fellowship with Him.

Yes, it is *then* that all this becomes a *conscious* reality to us, and we find ourselves singing with the happy Shulamith, "Lo, the winter is past; the flowers appear on the earth; and the time of the singing of the birds is come!" Is there anything for which Christian hearts have longed more wistfully than for such an unclouded fellowship with God, accompanied by a sense of continual cleansing?

There is one aspect of this text which used to puzzle me in my younger years. With the audacity of the novice I would fain have corrected John. I felt sure that those persons who "walk in the light" are the *least* in need of cleansing, and that it is those who walk in the darkness who most need it. Maturer experience corrected that misunderstanding. It is when we are walking in the light that we most clearly *see* our need of cleansing. This was brought home to me one lovely Spring day, years ago, when I was out for a pleasant tramp through the woods. I must have been in the woods two hours when I decided it was time to be making my way back to keep an appointment. Since I had trodden among ferns and mosses along by a stream, I looked down at my shoes and socks to see if I needed to call home for a clean-up, but all seemed respectable enough. Soon afterward, however, I strode from the twilight of the woods into an open meadow flooded with sunshine. For a moment the light was too strong and I lowered my eyes. When I did so, what a discovery! Bits of fern and moss and clay all over my shoes and trousers! I distinctly remember saying to myself, "Yes, it is when we come into the light that we most realize our need of cleansing!" What was unperceived amid the shade of the woods was painfully clear in the light!

Do I happen to be addressing someone who rather complacently says, "Well, I'm trying to live a good Christian life; I am not of the worldly sort; nor am I aware of anything badly wrong in my life; so I do not see any special need for cleansing"? Much as I dislike to say it, perhaps your complacence betrays that you are not "walking in the light as He is in the light". For to walk in *that* light so exposes hitherto unsuspected sin that at once we know acutely our need of cleansing. That is why, very often, the more we seek holiness the more unholy we feel. As the precious old hymn says,

> "And they who fain would serve Thee best
> Are conscious most of wrong within."

Thank God, when we really *do* "walk in the light as He is in the light" there *is* continuous cleansing through the propitiatory blood of the dear Saviour. But that raises the quite momentous question for us Christian believers: What does it *mean* to "walk in the light"?

The answer to that question is twofold. First, it means to walk with every known sinful or unworthy way of thinking, speaking, behaving, resolutely renounced. To the degree in which we allow compromise with what we know is morally wrong there is shadow across our fellowship with God. To that degree we are in the dark; and guidance from the Holy Spirit to our own spirit is blurred.

This matter of a resolute break-away from all that is unholy seems a desolating problem to some Christians. In helpless self-commiseration they exclaim, "Oh, if only I *could* break free from these evils which defeat me and frustrate my fellowship with God! But I *cannot*; they are an hereditary *part* of me. I simply cannot dislodge them. They are somehow innate in my very constitution by inheritance through our family bloodstream. I can no more detach them from my moral nature than I can detach my facial features from what I am physically."

It may be a comfort to some such believers if we point out that in so lamenting they are misapprehending what is required of them. Our obligation to renounce decidedly all that is known to be wrong refers *only* to that area of our life which is under the control of our *will*. Those evil proclivities of ours, such as proneness to envy, jealousy, lust, temper, selfishness, which inhere in our very nature through our birth into Adam's fallen race—*those* inborn evils you and I simply *cannot* expel from our being. They are not in that area where our *will* has the power to admit or to repulse. Our will can neither eject them nor change them. Only *God* can deal with *them*; and, thank God, there is provision against them in the Gospel message of sanctification through the Holy Spirit's transforming renewal of our minds (see Romans 12: 2, Ephesians 4: 23).

So, let it be clearly understood that when we refer to the neces-

sity of a resolute break from whatever we know to be sinful or
unworthy, we are referring only to that area of our life and being
over which the *will* has dominion—our choices, friendships,
habits, voluntary thoughts, ambitions, purposes, motives, ways
of speaking and behaving. Throughout the whole of that territory
there must be complete yieldedness to the sceptre of our royal
Master, and an accompanying intolerance of all that would grieve
or dishonour Him. *That,* in its first meaning, is "walking in the
light, as He is in the light"—walking with every evil way renounced.

Now although that is limited to the sphere in which the *will*
governs, it penetrates very deeply into the inner world of mind
and feeling. For instance, to mention only one subtle aspect, take
the matter of *grudges*. To "walk in the light as He is in the light"
means that I dare not hug even one sweet, darling personal grudge
against any other human being. Perhaps I should have put an
exclamation mark after that, for to some it will seem like the
knock-out blow to any possibility of entire sanctification. What!
not *one* grudge, when some grudges at least are so cruelly provoked, so amply deserved, so reasonable, so natural, so relieving
to the mind?

Well, let us see. We call ourselves followers of Jesus. If we are,
where do His dear sandal-prints lead us? See Him before Pilate,
already bruised and discoloured by rough-handling. See Him
scourged till He collapses at the last stroke of that fearful lash. See
Him mocked by Herod's men-at-arms. See Him staggering out
through the city gates bearing that heavy beam and transom. Will
He make it to the top of that knoll? See Him there, on Golgotha.
He is flung down on His back, and as He lies there iron spikes are
hammered through His hands. Then His feet are crossed, and a
larger spike is driven through both, fastening them to the wood.
Then half a dozen soldiers hoist aloft the cross with Him nailed
to it. A hole has been made in the ground into which the cross
and its suspended Victim are jolted in an upright position. Suddenly every vein is a swollen river of anguish; every nerve
is a strand of fire. The torture is excruciating. The Sufferer
cries out in the awful pain of it. And what is His gasping cry?
—"Father! . . . forgive . . . them; they know not . . . what
they do."

Oh, think again of that cry from that Cross! You say you are
a follower of *HIM,* yet you dare indulge the carnal luxury of

hugging a grudge! Oh, what condemnation that fearful yet sublime Cross flashes upon us and our wretched retaliations! In the light of that forlorn but resplendent self-sacrifice, and the dear, dear Saviour who hangs bleeding, how can we fondly nurse *any* secret spite?—or anything else which grieves His loving heart? No, no; we cannot coddle resentments, animosities, grudges and be the followers of Jesus. Nor can we house any other unholy lodger in our minds if we would "walk in the light as *He* is in the light".

To sum up: walking in the light means (1) to walk with all known sinning in thought, word, deed, resolutely renounced; (2) to live with our heart and life completely thrown open to God. Well may our prayer be,

> I ask, dear Lord,
>   A heart renewed and clean
> Reflecting Thee
>   With not a cloud between;
> A heart all Thine
> My King divine,
>   With holy love aglow;
> In me, dear Lord,
>   A heart like Thine bestow.

But now let us consider briefly some of the *precious benefits* which are ours when we "walk in the light". Look again at those words, "If we walk . . . *we have* . . ." What pages might be filled telling all that "we *have*" when we "walk in the light"! Two of its rewards are mentioned in the text, but there are many others implied along with those two. Let me touch on just a few.

The Way of Safety

To begin with, walking in the light ensures *safety*. Years ago I had a friend who was a city councillor. On one occasion he told me that statistics which were put before the City Council demonstrated that nearly all the nocturnal crime in that city was committed in streets which were insufficiently lighted. How true it is: there is safety in the light; there is danger in the dark! When I was a wee laddie, the jewellers' shops in our town all had heavy, iron-studded doors and window-shutters; and when the jewellers used to shut shop at nights they would fasten those heavy doors and shutters with big padlocks. Nowadays, when I return there,

I see the same shops, but the heavy barricades are all gone. Between all that glittering jewellery and the public there is just one thin sheet of plate-glass, and even the shop-door is now another glass window. The cumbersome padlocks are no more. All that the jeweller now does when he closes shop at nights is to turn a small key in the inconspicuous Yale lock, and *leave all the lights on!* Then, if "burglar Bill" comes prowling round, the *light* immediately exposes him to the watchful eye of the law!

Yes, there is safety in the light; there is danger in the dark. What is true in the physical world is equally true in the moral and spiritual. When there is prayerlessness, carelessness, compromise, toleration of doubtful things in our life, there is spiritual half-light or shadowy dusk. Temptations to evil stride into the mind, and it is difficult to detect their real identity. We are not sure whether some things are white or black; they seem a sort of middle grey. Often, therefore, we are deceived and become the Tempter's prey. We are tripped, robbed, cheated, and made to suffer by a traitor mistaken as an innocent. But when we are truly "walking in the light as He is in the light", as soon as anything sinful comes before the eyes of the mind its ugliness is exposed; we see it as what it really is, and in the strength of the Lord we say, "Get thee hence, Satan!"

How often have Christian believers come to me, and asked, "Do you think it is right for me to do this thing?" "Am I within Christian bounds, going to that place?" "Is such a friendship proper?" I always listen sympathetically and try to advise wisely, but deep in my heart I know that in about seven or eight instances out of every ten there would be no need to ask such questions if only the questioner were "walking in the light". It is wonderful how such questions answer themselves, or else never need to be asked, when we are "walking in the light". That is the one way of safety.

The Secret of Influence

But again, when we "walk in the light" we have the fullest *influence* for Christ. In the town of Romford, Essex, England, there used to be a Baptist minister named John Ewing. He was a man of quite ordinary public ability; not the type of speaker to be invited to special "occasions"; nothing of the glamorous about him whatever. Yet under his ministry the little church gradually grew from being a handful into the largest and most vigorous

Christian testimony for miles around. His unusual influence was due to two main factors. (1) Week in, week out, he steadily taught the Bible—taught it as only those can who hold it to be in its entirety the authentic Word of God. (2) Every time he came into the pulpit, he gave the distinct impression—as one after another told me—of having come straight from an audience with God. I came to know some of his closest colleagues and each said the same thing: if ever a man "walked in the light", John Ewing did. That was the secret of his influence.

When my dear wife and I were still in our 'teens, and were newly converted to Christ, we had a dear elderly friend whom we used to visit, and from whom we received much wise counsel in the faith. He was an undertaker, which, of course, meant that he had much contact with sorrow and mourning; but he himself was a radiant Christian full of good humour. Incidentally, he was rather sensitive about being an undertaker; so, as he once confided to me, whenever he was away on vacation, if anybody asked him, "Mr. Taylor, what is *your* vocation in life?" he used to reply, "Well, I *follow* the medical profession"! However, I am referring to him for something he told me about Dr. John Henry Jowett of Carrs Lane, Birmingham. Dr. Jowett was the greatest word-artist of the English pulpit at that time (some sixty years ago), but he was *more* than that, as old Mr. Taylor's story exemplifies.

George Taylor was anxious to win for the Saviour a certain tobacconist friend of his in Birmingham. He got the idea that if only he could take him to hear Jowett, that tobacconist might get converted. It took much persuasion, but he succeeded in getting him there one Sunday morning. The church was completely full. George Taylor and his friend sat in the right-hand gallery. Soon the service began. When the fresh-complexioned, shining-faced Jowett entered the pulpit and bowed in prayer, the tobacconist seemed taken aback. He fixed an almost incredulous gaze on the man of God, and kept it there all through the service. When the congregation stood to sing a hymn, the man just silently stared at Jowett. When Jowett led the congregation in prayer, this man, with eyes still open, just kept looking at Jowett. So it was, all the time Jowett preached, and through the final hymn. On the way home not a remark was made between Mr. Taylor and his friend —not until they came to the street corner where they parted. Then, just as they left each other, the tobacconist said, with husky-voiced emotion, "Taylor, that man in that pulpit *made me feel filthy*. I'll never sell tobacco again as long as I live." And he never did; for the very next morning, in the window of his large tobacconist store, there was a notice, "These Premises for Sale!"

Jowett's almost seraphic influence was a by-product of "walking in the light". Those who *continually* "walk in the light", through the years, gradually contract and reflect the light which streams from the Saviour's face; even as Moses, after his long-ago "forty days and forty nights" of communion with God on Sinai, returned to the camp of Israel with his very face aglow. Have we not all known consecrated believers, praying saints, who lived on the doorstep of heaven, whose very personalities were *atmosphered* in the Holy Spirit, and whose diffused influence was nothing less than benign?

Fellowship with God

Next, it is when we "walk in the light as He is in the light" that we have fellowship with God. Such fellowship is the sweetest mystery and most exalted privilege in all the universe. That is equally true whether it be said of the cherubim or of first-rank angels or of men or of any other order of beings. *No* privilege can eclipse that—which makes our average neglect of it all the stranger. Oh, richly happy are those human hearts which, through habitual fellowship with God, have become shrines of the Spirit's continuous indwelling! Theirs is a soaring joy utterly unintelligible to this present raucous age, and, alas, unknown by all too many professing Christians.

During the pre-war years of my ministry in Edinburgh, Scotland, I frequently travelled by train between the Scottish capital and London, England. There are several long tunnels on that run; and I always used to notice that however busily engaged in conversation all of us passengers were, in the eight-seater compartments, as soon as the train rushed us into the darkness of a long tunnel the conversation was suddenly suspended. Conversation is not easy in a darkness which prevents people from seeing each other. Just the same is true in this matter of spiritual fellowship. Where darkness interferes with face-to-face converse there cannot be real fellowship with God. We must come right into the light, and then keep "*walking* in the light as He is in the light". Then, as drooping flowers gratefully open to the morning sun, we find those purest, sweetest joys awaking within us which this world can neither give nor take away.

Continuous Cleansing

Another precious accompaniment of walking in the light is the continuous *cleansing* which is promised in our text. In my recently published book, *A New Call to Holiness,* I have tried to show, on exegetical grounds, that the cleansing indicated in 1 John 1: 7 is not an inward cleansing of the *heart,* but a *judicial* cleansing from sin as *guilt*. Never once in Scripture is blood used of either inwardly or outwardly cleansing a person. Always, in the actual cleansing of a person or object, the cleansing element is not blood but *water,* a type of the Holy Spirit. That is why Paul says, in Ephesians 5: 25, "Christ also loved the Church, and gave Himself for it, that He might sanctify it, having *cleansed* it by the washing of *water* with the Word." That is why he says in Titus 3: 5. 6, "According to His mercy He saved us, through the *washing* of regeneration and renewing of the Holy Spirit . . ." Any inward cleansing or renewing which is *ever* effected in you or me is our Lord's work in us by the Holy Spirit. The Cross of Calvary is the procuring *cause,* but the Holy Spirit is the effecting *Agent*.

What, then, more specifically, is the cleansing denoted in 1 John 1: 7? Well, it is truer to the original, in my judgment, if we translate the Greek word, *pas,* as "every" rather than "all"— i.e. "cleanseth from *every* sin". Indeed, that is how *Young's Literal Translation,* and the *Twentieth Century New Testament,* and Moffatt, and others translate it. If we "walk in the light as He is in the light", the Calvary atonement continually answers for us before God, cleansing away, to the very last spot, all stain of guilt before the holy eyes of God, and at the same time cleansing our own conscience from all *sense* of guilt which could mar or block our fellowship with God.

The fact is, when we "walk in the light" we begin to recognise as sins things which we never before perceived or even suspected were sins. Thus we sense, as never before, our *need* of this continuous cleansing before God; and at the same time we experience with new depth the *reality* of it. The whole precious wonder of it becomes luminous to the mind. With a glowing vividness never known before, we realize the meaning of a cleansed *conscience* (Heb. 10: 22), and the Holy Spirit makes real within us an experience of open fellowship with the heavenly Father without one impeding shadow between Him and our own hearts.

Oh, the deep, rich wonder of it,
    Gone, all guilt and stain and fear!
And the smile of God, like sunrise
    Breaks upon me full and clear!

Heavenly Guidance

Then again, one of the things which we naturally want to emphasize here is, that walking in the light brings heavenly *guidance* into our earthly walk. This has been the main emphasis all through this chain of studies. We might almost summarize the whole in two comprehensive propositions: (1) divine guidance is clearly promised to us in the Bible; (2) walking in the light is the prerequisite of our receiving it.

Guidance which would be quite easy in daylight is often awkward to communicate at night. One evening, not long since, a stranger asked me if I could direct him to a certain address in a large suburb. I knew fairly well the place he wanted to find, but I had to say to him, "If only you had asked me in daylight it would have been ten times easier to direct you." As I spoke to him I found myself inwardly musing, "Quite so: guidance easier in the light than in the dark—another instance in which what is true of the physical world is true in the spiritual." Many Christians wonder, from time to time, why urgently sought guidance seems withheld or indeterminate, when all the while the fault is on their own side, and the explanation is that they are not "walking in the light as *He* is in the light". Let this be underscored in our thinking: even God cannot guide us easily or clearly when we are not walking in the light.

Conversely, when we *do* "walk in the light", there *is* heavenly guidance. It is guidance of a new kind which few, even among believers, seem to know, except perhaps in broken periods. I mean guidance, not just given in reply to our much beseeching but continuously communicated as a part of our *fellowship* with God. The understanding between God and the consecrated heart is so unclouded that the Father's will is all the while making itself real —yes, real to the point where *asking* for it to be made known is often needless. In this heart-to-heart communion, the Holy Spirit, moment by moment, gently but unmistakably impresses the

Father's leading upon the spiritual sensitivity of the human mind which is living and walking "in the light". Oh, it is a friendship with God which above all blessings of the earth should be coveted by us Christian believers!

The Joy Unspeakable

We might continue for a long time expatiating on the blessings which come to those who "walk in the light as He is in the light", but we mention only one more. Walking in the light brings *joy*. I emphasize that word, "joy", as distinct from mere happiness or pleasure, which is more or less determined by circumstances. *Joy* is not dependent upon the unstable exteriorities of our earthly life. It is a well of living water deep down in the soul of its possessor. When we have truly found it through a heart-to-heart experience of Christ, we begin to sing dear old stanzas with new meaning—

> I've found a joy in sorrow,
> A secret balm for pain,
> A beautiful tomorrow
> Of sunshine after rain;
> I've found a branch of healing
> Near every bitter spring,
> A whispered promise stealing
> O'er every broken thing!

All this becomes ours in maximum experience when we "walk in the light as He is in the light". Weights become wings! Burdens become blessings! Difficulties become opportunities! Sighs become songs! There is light amid gloom. Sorrow brings a secret new stairway to the Father's sympathy. There are streams in the desert, and songs in the night, and springs in the valleys; and our deserts of arid circumstance blossom as the rose. Persecution, sickness, the ominous morrow, heavy seas of trial, all cease to affright. How to explain it to someone who has never experienced it is beyond us. All we know is, that as we "walk in the light as He is in the light", fear, with its torment, is gone, and we can genuinely say with the psalmist,

> "We will not fear though the earth do change,
> Though the mountains be shaken into the heart of the seas."

Even tears no longer have bitterness. Nay, on the contrary, we find Jesus loveliest and dearest of all when we see Him through our earthly tears. The will of God is no longer merely something to *bear*; a chain which chafes us; an iron fixity which we knuckle under with regret. Oh, no! we now wonder that we could ever have been so blind to it as we were before. We *glory* in it. We see in it all the gracious wisdom of the heavenly Father's boundless love for us, directing, permitting, and sovereignly overruling, so that "all things work together for good to them that love God, to them who are the called according to His purpose" (Rom. 8: 28). The cup which our Father has given us, shall we not drink it? Beyond every cross we now see a gleaming crown. Our song is that of Philip Doddridge,

> My gracious Lord, I own thy right
> To every service I can pay,
> And call it my *supreme delight*
> To hear Thy dictates and obey.

All this may seem like florid exaggeration to those believers who walk in the dusky dimness of a *part*-yieldedness and part self-retention, with a fluctuating spiritual experience and a patchy prayer-life; but those who are God's twentieth-century Enochs, who "walk with God" in the light of unsullied communion, know indeed how *un*exaggeratedly true it is.

To all the Lord's children who chance on these pages we say, in the words of Isaiah 2: 5, "O house of Jacob, come ye, and *let us walk in the light of Jehovah.*" Did you know that walking is the commonest of all the New Testament metaphors for the Christian life? What *is* a walk? It has been defined as "a reiterated first step". Every walk must begin with a "first step"; then that first step becomes a walk by reiteration. Even so, if you and I would "walk in the light as He is in the light", there must be that first step *into* the light. Be not deceived: there simply *cannot* be any true walking in the light apart from that "first step" *into* it. That first step is a glad, resolute, utter yielding to Christ. That, and that alone, is the proof that He is supreme in our heart's love. That, and that alone, gives Him unobstructed right of way in our life. That, and that alone, gives Him full opportunity to "manifest" Himself to us (John 14: 21). That, and that alone, brings the promised infilling by the Holy Spirit. That, and that alone, brings continuous *guidance* and the "joy unspeakable".

My glad and utter yieldedness
His royal heart demands,
My King of Love, all loveliness,
With nail-scars in His hands:
And dare I yield Him but a part?
How can I but adore,
And yield my will, my very heart,
To Him for evermore?

Yes, that is "the first step", and once we have taken it we are to follow it up with daily, hourly, momently *reiteration,* so that the step becomes a *walk*; the initial crisis becomes a sanctifying process; and that which seemed so hard, so costly to "the flesh", at the outset, becomes the glad, natural, reposeful *attitude* of our mind. *That* is "walking in the light as He is in the light", and it brings a supernal joy of heart which can only be expressed in such words as Isaiah 60: 19, 20,

"THE SUN SHALL BE NO MORE THY LIGHT BY DAY; NEITHER FOR BRIGHTNESS SHALL THE MOON GIVE LIGHT UNTO THEE: BUT THE LORD SHALL BE UNTO THEE AN EVERLASTING LIGHT, AND THY GOD THY GLORY. THY SUN SHALL NO MORE GO DOWN: NEITHER SHALL THY MOON WITHDRAW ITSELF: FOR THE LORD SHALL BE THINE EVERLASTING LIGHT, AND THE DAYS OF THY MOURNING SHALL BE ENDED."

POSTSCRIPT: WHY NOT YOU?

The humblest followers of Jesus may know the divine will at first hand. It is every man's privilege to be fully assured in the will of God. The Divine attention to detail is amazing. Nothing is too trivial for Omniscience.

Samuel Chadwick.

Our thought of God here is not too human; the reasoning of our critics is that. He is not a smaller God who astounds the astronomer with His mathematical universe, and at the same time answers the cry of the burdened heart and speaks peace to the penitent soul. He is a greater God, such a God as Jesus revealed and before whom the angels veil their faces. Though He is far, far above our thought, we dare believe that He stoops to ask the love of our poor hearts: though whirling worlds move at His word, we dare believe that He said, "I will guide thee." "Be still and *know* that I am God."

W. E. Sangster.

"He is not far from any one of us"
Acts 17: 27 (A.S.V.).

12

POSTSCRIPT: WHY NOT YOU?

FROM time to time in the foregoing chapters we have emphasized the importance of making the inspired Scriptures the touchstone of divine guidance; and we would underscore that again here. Yet it may be that we have not given full enough reference to the ministry of the *Holy Spirit* as the Executive or direct Communicator of guidance to the mind of the Christian believer. Nor, perhaps, have we sufficiently stressed the truly *consecrated life,* as that prerequisite which, on the human side, makes it possible for the Spirit's guidance to break on the mind full and clear. So, let this postscript briefly but earnestly correct that lack, if needed, by a concentrated emphasis in these final paragraphs.

If we are meant to take the Acts of the Apostles as our pattern (and in this I think we *are*), then we ought to observe carefully three features belonging to Spirit-given guidance as it then came in anew with the Christian dispensation: (1) it was an indubitable reality, (2) it gave unerring initiative and direction, (3) it operated only through consecrated, Spirit-filled, prayerful men and women. Reflect on these three aspects for a few moments.

First, guidance by the Holy Spirit was a conspicuous *reality.* Nothing is more remarkable in that Christianity of the first days than the operation of the supernatural through the natural; of divine guidance to and through guidable human persons. It is vividly stamped upon every page of the Acts, from that first historic "day of Pentecost" onwards; and the whole record is written in suchwise as to *seem,* at least, like an intended "original" of what may be *continually* expected to occur through Spirit-filled Christian believers.

Here and there, in the Acts, the guidance is unexpected and surprising; as, for instance, the sudden directing of Philip away from the Samaria revival to the Gaza desert, to intercept the Ethiopian chancellor (8: 26), or the Spirit's "forbidding" Paul to "preach the Word in Asia" (16: 6) and "suffering them not" to go "into Bithynia" (16: 7).

The vital *strategy* of receiving and obeying such direct guidance is exemplified in that latter instance. The diverting of Paul and his little group from Asia and Bithynia proved to be one of the greatest turning-points in human history. It brought the Gospel to Europe. At that time, to human eyes, it must have seemed far more worthwhile to go to populous Asia or fertile Bithynia than "way out West" to what must have looked like the outer edge of things. Perhaps Paul, that master missionary-statesman, was puzzled. Little did he or any other human being know just then how the centre of the civilized world was to gravitate in that northern and western direction, and that a little group of islands furthest out of all was to become the hub of the widest-spreading empire ever known. But the omniscient divine Spirit foreknew all, and guided accordingly.

Two thousand years have slipped away since then; the world background has vastly changed; and the whole face of life wears very different features; but has that guidance which belonged to the first days folded up? Have we any valid reason for presuming so? Are we not still in the "age of grace" which came in at Pentecost? Is not this age of grace in a unique way the "dispensation of the Spirit"? Has the once-for-all immersion of the whole Church in the Holy Spirit (1 Cor. 12: 13) exhausted itself? Although many of the abnormal "sign-miracles" to *Israel,* such as spectacular healings and raisings of the dead, have dropped away as no longer relevant now that the "kingdom" offer to Israel is suspended, has the Holy Spirit Himself been withdrawn from the *Church*? Although the passing centuries have greatly reshaped the externals of human society, is supernatural guidance no longer necessary?

One has only to ask such questions to know the answer. If there is a *lack* of realized guidance today, the reason is to be sought elsewhere. A significant clue to the change between then and now may be found in a quite incidental sentence which occurs in Acts 15, in connection with the first ecumenical Christian council ever held. When the leaders of that "assembly" wrote an official letter to the Gentiles concerning their relation to the Mosaic law, they used these words at one point,

"FOR IT SEEMED GOOD TO THE HOLY SPIRIT AND TO US. . . ." (28).

If anything could strikingly indicate the dominance of the Holy Spirit in that Christianity of the first days, it is the utterly natural and incidental way in which the Spirit's leadership is mentioned in that twenty-eighth verse. The supernatural working through the natural had become the normal and expected.

But that twenty-eighth verse also gives the *key* to that experience of continual guidance. Note the order of the wording. Those early leaders did *not* say, "It seemed good unto us and to the Holy Spirit" (putting the "us" before the "Spirit"), but, "It seemed good to the *Holy Spirit* and to us." They most naturally wrote it that way because they *lived* it that way. They were men yielded to Christ without a fleck of reserve, and they were therefore men wholly at the *disposal* of the Holy Spirit. From then until now the decisive factor has remained the same: the fully *yielded* are the fully *guided*.

That brings me to my final accent. Yieldedness and guidedness and continual *prayerfulness* always go together in the operation of the Holy Spirit through Christian believers. So, let my parting emphasis be on consecration and prayer. We often talk with flowing ease about consecration to Christ; but how few of us really live the *life* of utter Christ-monopoly! In Acts 15: 26, Paul and Barnabas are described as "men that have hazarded their lives for the Name of our Lord Jesus Christ". Translated with strict literalness it is, "men who have *handed over* their souls". Something of what that complete hand-over meant, of risk and reward, of labour and joy unspeakable, of trouble and triumph, of being blessed and used and guided and guarded, we know. That utter hand-over is the supreme, post-conversion crisis in *any* Christian life, and it brings the touch of immortality into everything which we say or do for Christ thereafter. From that point onwards, also, there is a *guidedness* operating all through our life which gives everything new significance.

Yes, this out-and-out hand-over to Christ is the all-determining factor; and I want to mention four things about it.

First: the *ground* of such consecration is our Lord's *ownership* of us. He loved us (oh, the mystery of it!). He bought us (oh, the cost of it). He owns us (what further right have we to self-management?). As 1 Corinthians 6: 19, 20, says, "Ye are not your own. For ye are bought with a price: therefore glorify God in your body and in your spirit, *which are God's.*"

Second: the *motive* of such consecration must be our *love* for Christ: love of Him for what He has suffered and done for us; love of Him for what He is in Himself, even the "altogether lovely"; love of Him for what He has become to us in our varying experiences of life; love for Him which is now so deep that we cannot bear the thought of *anything* coming between Him and us; love which finds its purest joy in bringing glory to such a dear, dear Saviour. No other motive can be so warm and strong and enduring.

Third: the *inspiration* of such consecration is, that in response to our loving and grateful and entire "hand-over" of ourselves to His monopoly, He takes us and sanctifies us by a thorough-going inward renewal of our mind in all its desires, motives, inclinations; that in His own way He fills the surrendered human vessel with the Holy Spirit; that He guides and guards and blesses and uses us to His own gracious ends, and that we know the wonder of that heart-to-heart fellowship which is indicated in John 14: 21—"He that hath My commandments and keepeth them, he it is that loveth Me; and He that loveth Me shall be loved of my Father; and I will love him, and will *manifest Myself to him.*"

Fourth: the *reward* of such consecration is, that in addition to the joy of present sanctification and heart-deep fellowship with Him, and utmost present usefulness to Him, there shall be the *overcomer's crown* at last—that ultimate, enrapturing destiny of *highest* service in the Beyond, for which *only* an utter consecration here on earth can prepare us. "He that overcometh shall inherit all these things" (Rev. 21: 7).

Dear fellow-believer whom I now have the privilege of addressing in the Name which we all dearly love, let it sink down deeply into your soul: the most vital and far-reaching post-conversion crisis in *any* believer's life is this *utter* self-yielding to Christ. You may hold this or that or the other theory of sanctification; you may hold this or that or the other theory about the so-called "baptism in the Holy Spirit"; you may hold the "pre" or the "post" or the "mid" theory about the so-called "great tribulation" and the "secret rapture of the Church"; but the only thing which will fling open the gates to what Paul calls "the *fulness* of the blessing" (Rom. 15: 29) is this glad and adoring and *total* surrender to the will of our glorious Lord Jesus; a self-yielding *actually* (and not merely wishfully) transacted, and followed by a life of regular, daily lingerings in secret communion with Him.

Oh, that is the "life more abundant", with its "joy unspeakable", and its "peace which passeth all understanding", and its "wisdom from above", and its "enduement with power from on high", and its "always abounding", and its "bringing forth much fruit". And that is the continually *guided* life. Intermittent guidance, or crisis-guidance now and then by special "signs", may come to many others in answer to emergency pleadings; but, a *life* of guidance, an experience of *direct and continual* guidance from the Holy Spirit to our own tuned-in sensitivity, belongs only to the entirely consecrated and Christ-possessed. Therefore this post-script appeal is for nothing less than *that* response to Him; and we finish our little book in prostrate adoration at His feet.

> Could deeper, higher wonder ever be?—
> That *He*, creation's King, for love of me
> Once left His throne ineffable, and came
> To hang upon a felon's cross of shame!
>
> Or was there ever costlier purchase-price
> Than that astounding, vast Self-sacrifice,
> To set a guilty sin-bound captive free,
> And open Paradise, at last, to me?
>
> Oh, mighty splendour of that Easter day!
> Love all-triumphant rolls the stone away!
> By Calv'ry purchase, Saviour, I am Thine;
> And now, in resurrection, Thou art mine!
>
> O thorn-crowned Saviour-King whom I adore,
> Find in my heart an ever-open door;
> Make now my will a highway for Thine own;
> Let all my days fulfil Thy will alone.
>
> Henceforth may no self-schemings intervene
> To dim the "heavenly vision" I have seen;
> But all my grateful heart so yielded be
> That life may be a *guided walk* with Thee.